BUSINESS/SCIENCE/TECHNOLOGY DIVISION
CHICAGO PUBLIC LIBRARY
400 SOUTH STATE STREET
CHICAGO, IL 60605

W9-DDQ-748

Chicago Public Library

REFERENCE

Form 178 rev. 1-94

CHICAGO PUBLIC LIBRARY
CHICAGO, IL. 60605

G. & D. COOK & CO.'s

Illustrated Catalogue of Carriages and Special Business Advertiser

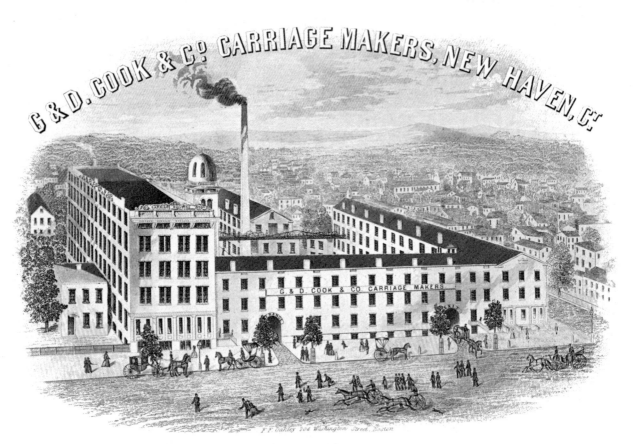

G & D. COOK & Cº CARRIAGE MAKERS, NEW HAVEN, Cº

G. & D. COOK & CO. CARRIAGE MAKERS

J. F. Oakley 104 Washington Street, Boston

GEORGE COOK.   DAVID COOK.   H. I. KIMBALL.

DOVER *Pictorial Archive* SERIES

G. & D. COOK & CO.'s
Illustrated Catalogue of Carriages and Special Business Advertiser

with a new Foreword by
PAUL H. DOWNING

DOVER PUBLICATIONS, INC., NEW YORK

Ref
TS
2033
.C6
1970

Copyright © 1970 by Dover Publications, Inc.
All rights reserved under Pan American and International Copyright Conventions.

Published in Canada by General Publishing Company, Ltd., 30 Lesmill Road, Don Mills, Toronto, Ontario.
Published in the United Kingdom by Constable and Company, Ltd., 10 Orange Street, London WC 2.

This Dover edition, first published in 1970, is an unabridged and unaltered republication of the work originally published by G. & D. Cook and Company in 1860.
This reprint contains a new Foreword by Paul H. Downing.

This book belongs to the Dover Pictorial Archive Series. Up to ten illustrations may be reproduced on any one project or in any single publication, free and without special permission. Wherever possible include a credit line indicating the title of this book and publisher. Please address the publisher for permission to make more extensive use of the illustrations in this book than that authorized above.
The republication of this book in whole is prohibited.

Standard Book Number: 486-22364-7
Library of Congress Catalog Card Number: 74-105523

Manufactured in the United States of America
Dover Publications, Inc.
180 Varick Street
New York, N.Y. 10014

BUSINESS ~~~~~~~~~ TECHNOLOGY DIVISION
CHICAGO PUBLIC LIBRARY
400 SOUTH STATE STREET
CHICAGO, IL 60605

R0119628426

Foreword to the Dover Edition

WHILE it is true that some of the more delicate arts imported to America from the Old World suffered in the hands of Colonial craftsmen, it is also a fact that the more practical crafts were, as a rule, greatly improved by our industrious forebears. Look, for example, at the gunsmiths of Pennsylvania who perfected the "Kentucky" rifle, which shot truer than European counterparts and which also used much less powder.

The horse drawn vehicle is an excellent example of a device which was developed and improved by Americans. As traffic in America began to shift from rivers to roads in the mid-1800's, American carriage manufacturers, in order to economize horse power, invented machines that shaped tough and springy native woods—whitewood from the tulip tree, and hickory—into the lightest of durable carriages. The spidery wheels that frightened Europeans withstood our rough roads thanks to precisely machined spokes fitted into precisely drilled hub mortises, all enclosed in steel tires set by steam power.

This extraordinary technical ability tempted some designers to be genteel to the point of flossiness in concocting family coaches that the Smiths purchased to outdo the Joneses, but the strictly practical buckboards, buggies and surreys, on the other hand, are designed with a spareness as elegant as that which characterizes Shaker furniture. Such simplicity fits today's belief that less is more.

Since only a few of our old carriages have survived in scattered museums, the catalog here reprinted is now one of the most important and comprehensive sources of information on these vehicles. In 1860 the firm of G. and D. Cook and Company was the largest carriage manufactory in the world; working on an assembly-line system, it turned out a solidly built vehicle every hour of the working day. At the end of this volume two charming essays report the history and methods of that eminent establishment and the character of life in bustling New Haven immediately prior to the Civil War. The Introduction, with its earnest exposition of the company's policies and procedures, is of interest as a candid first-hand view of America in the heyday of the Mechanical Age—its steam engines working at full speed, its craftsmen busily employed in ever better and more productive labor, its Connecticut Yankee citizens confident of obtaining ever increasing advantages from man's genius for invention, organization and commerce. This confidence and optimism is very much evident in the charming advertisements which accompany the plates and which make the volume an historical social document as well as a comprehensive catalog of carriages.

PAUL H. DOWNING

Staten Island, New York, October, 1969

Buyer of Stock & Material.

Corresponding & Financial Manager.

Salesman & General Manager of Manufactory.

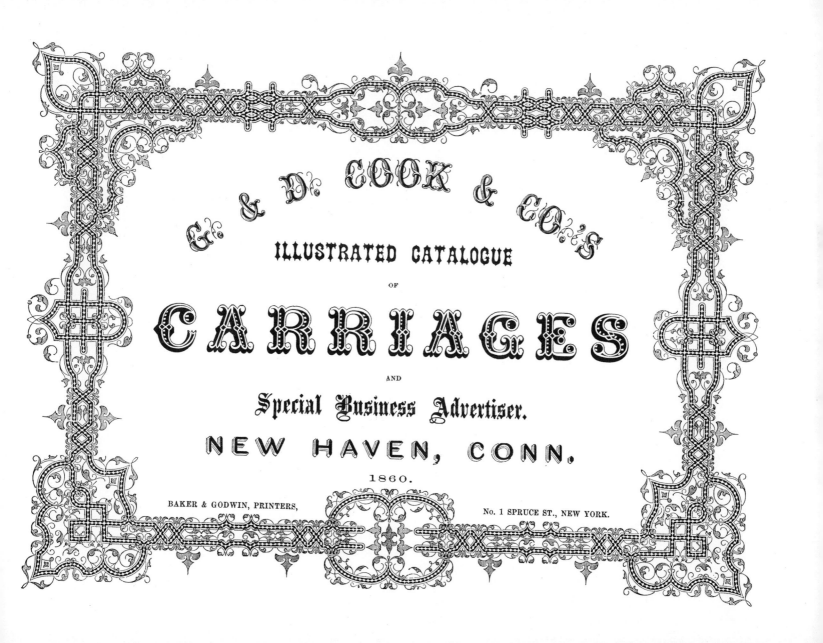

G. & D. COOK & CO.'S

ILLUSTRATED CATALOGUE

OF

CARRIAGES

AND

Special Business Advertiser.

NEW HAVEN, CONN.

1860.

BAKER & GODWIN, PRINTERS,

No. 1 SPRUCE ST., NEW YORK.

INTRODUCTION.

The Great Center of North American trade and travel is doubtless New York. The necessities of business, no less than all the resources of a high civilization, compel from distant trades and travelers the willing tribute of a visit to its teeming streets, where life flows so full and so condensed.

But men of business, however restricted or comprehensive their operations may be, greatly need to know the real commercial, manufacturing, and other interests and advantages, not only of New York, but of every considerable town and section of the country; its population, its business relations and connections with other large towns and sections, as well as with New York,—what Steamboats, Sailing Vessels, and Railroads it has, and most of all to know what direction the activity and genius of the people has taken; what they are really doing; what they make, and have to sell; what and how much they want to *buy*; how much, how promptly, and in what way they can *pay*, as well as the *names* of some of these men with whom they can safely deal; and in fine, what can be had, and seen, and bought, and sold, that altogether make up the solid pecuniary advantages, and the incidental pleasures, that a visit to it, or a correspondence with it, will yield.

In presenting to the public this second edition of our "*Descriptive Carriage Chart*," it has been our aim to give, in an authentic and reliable form, as much of this information relative to New Haven and vicinity, as our space would allow. And to accomplish this we have deemed it desirable that a large variety of trades and occupations other than our own, should be herein represented. Accordingly we have obtained, and upon the various pages of this book will be found, the *Business Cards* of some of the most extensive and reliable Houses, in their line, to be found in the country, all pointing to different branches of commercial and industrial pursuits.

For a more extended view of the city, its surroundings, and social and business interests and relations, we refer you to an article from the pen of an eminent New Haven writer, which we have inserted in the latter part of this book.

We desire and intend to scatter this information far and wide, so that any person in this broad land, whether in Illinois, in Georgia, or in California, with this book before him, may be able at once to form a just conception both of our city and of our *business*, and to judge whether a visit to our establishment, or to our beautiful " *City of Elms*," may advance his real pecuniary interests, or afford him a new gratification.

With these general remarks, we may be allowed to refer more at length to the details of our own business, and in so doing, it is no part of our plan to *boast* or to *exaggerate*. We mean simply to present a statement of such *facts* as we believe it will be for the interest of the Carriage dealers and consumers throughout the country to know. We expect many of them will visit us *personally*, and " *learn whether these things be so ;* " and indeed we deem it very desirable that they should, as it will afford them not only an opportunity of going through the establishment, and of examining the work in process of manufacture in the various departments, but of seeing the *quality* of stock and materials used, the *system* with which everything is managed, the care taken in the execution of orders, and of becoming personally acquainted with the *men* with whom they are to deal ; all of which, to the careful purchaser, are important considerations.

But knowing well that it is impossible that all who may want carriages can visit us in person, it has been our aim, in the preparation of this work, to present everything so *plainly*, that any one into whose hands it should come could readily understand just what kind of a carriage he would get by ordering any of the numerous styles herein represented. It is quite impossible, however, to give a minute description of all the varieties with which each may be finished. We give a representation of the average finish. Each style may be made plainer and cheaper than the representation, or more elegant, showy, and expensive. The qualities of Axles, Springs, Wheels, Plate, Cloth, Trimmings, and the other materials of which carriages are made, differ so widely, that the outward appearance does not *always* indicate the real value of the carriage ; for a very plain appearing one is often richer and more expensive than an elaborate and showy one. We intend always to *give each buyer the full value of his money, and then to let him decide where the special expense shall be put*, and in every way to fulfill every contract so thoroughly and so promptly, that *business* shall be a pleasure, not only to us, but to those with whom we deal.

With this plan, persons at a distance can feel safe in ordering any of the styles here represented, and be sure to *be served just as well as if they ordered in person*. Only be particular to state just how you want your carriage finished, whether plain or showy, heavy or light, hung high or low, about how much weight it is designed to carry, and whether your roads are hilly, hard, and stony, or level and sandy; also about the average width of track. In short, tell us all about what you *want*, and we have no hesitancy in saying *we can please you*.

Our facilities for the manufacturing of carriages are *to-day, greater than any other establishment in the world*, and we are constantly making new additions and improvements. Very much of our work, being done by *machinery*, is executed with a *precision and exactness* that cannot possibly be attained by hand labor. Our whole establishment is conducted not only upon an extensive scale, but with the most perfect *system ;*—our work being so arranged, divided and sub-divided, that each workman devotes his whole time and capacity to doing a single thing, and incidentally to devising new ways of doing that thing simpler, better and *cheaper*.

There is still another advantage derived from the systematic manner in which our work is done, aside from the fact of its being done better and cheaper; for if any part breaks, we can always supply its place with a new one that will fit as well as the original.

Or should you buy a no-top carriage and afterwards desire a top put on, we can send one at a day's notice that will fit perfectly. These are considerations of special importance to dealers, as they can always change tops, seats, bodies, backs, and in fact almost any part of a carriage, from one to another, and thus with but few carriages on hand at any one time, can make up a large variety.

With these advantages, and the many others (which we cannot here stop to mention), we feel confident we can make it for the advantage of purchasers to give us their trade, for we believe we can *safely* say, that no establishment in the *country*, or indeed in the *world*, can *successfully compete* with us in *quality, style, and price*.

The careful and correct forwarding, shipping, and insuring of carriages and other goods, are matters of the utmost importance to the purchaser, and in order to insure all this to our customers, we have established a forwarding and shipping agency in New York of our own, where not only goods purchased of us, but all merchandise whatsoever, is promptly forwarded to all parts of the country. For particulars, see pages 66 and 142 of this book.

DESCRIPTIVE PRICE LIST.

No. 1.—**Wide World.**   Price, from $115 to $140.

This style of Buggy is used in every part of the country where Buggies are used, is roomy, well-proportioned, and strong; can be finished with or without the Lazy Back; is usually finished plain, but calculated for service.

No. 2.—**Legion.**   Price, $115 to $140.

The most popular style of No Top Buggy in the South.   Very neat and genteel, and is usually finished fine and showy, with movable back and rack; boot creased, stitched, striped, or molded.

No. 3.—**The Gem.**   Price, $165 to $200.

Same as No. 1, with a shifting top, though it is represented as being more showily finished, with plated steps, silver molding on panel, &c.

No. 4.—**Pride of the South.**   Price, $145 to $180.

This is a very appropriate name for this Buggy, for with the Southern people it is a universal favorite, and is used in every section of the South.   Shifting top, with lever for raising and lowering the top from the inside; an acknowledged great improvement on the old way.   Full plated joints, rails, braces, &c.   Can be finished plain or fine, to suit.

No. 5.—**Queen's Phaeton.**   Price, $225 to $275.

A style peculiarly adapted for the use of old people, and greatly admired by the ladies.   Hangs low, and is easy of access. Five bow top, with spring lever; with high, comfortable, springy back; and for comfort, style, and beauty, this Buggy cannot be surpassed.   It is usually finished very fine, silver mounted, ornamented panels, &c., but looks very rich when finished plain.

No. 6.—**Box Jump Seat.**   Price, $185 to $235.

The best and most popular adjustable seat Buggy ever invented. Is roomy, light, and perfectly adapted for two or four persons, and can be instantaneously changed from a one to a two seat form and back.   Finished with a five bow shifting-top and hood, with spring lever for raising and falling; full plate, and neat ornaments.   This job, finished perfectly plain, is very tasty.   For full particulars and certificates, see page 32.

No. 6 B.—**Box Jump Seat.**

Same as No. 6, showing it in a two seat form.

No. 7.—**Philadelphia Top.**   Price, $165 to $200.

A style much used in Philadelphia, and has become a very popular vehicle.   Is usually finished plain, but light and very neat.

Paneled sides, and neatly ornamented leather dash, and a light, open, shifting top; spring lever.

No. 10.—Jocelyn No Top. Price, $140 to $175.

The Jocelyn Buggy, or very light no top, may be hung on cross or pole springs; is very light and durable for fast driving.

No. 11.—Philadelphia No Top. Price, $115 to $140.

Same as No. 7, but without top. Plain, neat, light, and comfortable.

No. 13.—Gipsy Top. Price, $170 to $205.

A style much in use at the North and West, and is fast becoming popular with the Southern people; and when finished fine it is one of the most attractive Buggies of the present day.

No. 15.—Concord Top. Price, $130 to $170.

This is a very good style, usually finished plain, with side springs, which are easy riding but not so well adapted for top Buggies as for no tops.

No. 16.—Georgia No Top. Price, $80 to $100.

This style is used extensively in Georgia, hence its name. Is made after the Concord style, on side springs, and is well liked as a cheap, durable Buggy.

No. 18.—Concord No Top. Price, $100 to $135.

This style first originated with the makers in Concord, N. H. From that city it takes its name. It is made in the very best manner, with case-hardened axles and English-steel springs. They are peculiarly adapted for hard use, and no Buggy runs easier, or rides better, and gives more general satisfaction than this style, if properly made. Is highly recommended, and in use in every part of the land.

No. 19.—Cane Side Buggy. Price, $185 to $215.

A light and tasty Buggy, much in use in the Northern and Western cities, though not as popular as it formerly was. Leather dash and shifting top. Is finished plain, but is neat and substantial.

No. 20. Price, $135 to $155.

Same as No. 19, but without top. Fine appearing, roomy, and light.

No. 21.—City No Top. Price, $135 to $155.

A deep side body, with iron dash, panels molded and striped, boot stitched and creased, plated steps and seat rail; or it may be finished perfectly plain black.

No. 22.—Sporting Wagon. Price, $140 to $175.

With deeper sides than No. 21, and more elegantly finished. It is universally admired for its elegance and beauty; is very roomy, but quite light.

No. 23.—City Top. Price, $185 to $220.

With body and carriage varying but little from No. 21. With light, shifting, five bow top, and is mostly used in cities, but is well adapted for any other use. Usually finished of the very best stock and finest workmanship.

No. 24.—**Tontine Top.** Price, $190 to $225.

Same as No. 22, with a top.

No. 25.—**Excelsior Top.** Price, $175 to $220.

A very graceful style, with painted boot and wood dash. Neatly ornamented, stirrup steps covered, plated rail and braces, shifting top, with lever attachment; with or without opera board. Similar to No. 4, but much finer finished.

No. 26.—**French Jump Seat.** Price, $160 to $200.

Similar in style to No. 6, with plated seat rail, or back, instead of top. Ornamental sides, double steps, plated iron dash, &c. Is adjusted from one to a two seat form, same as No. 6.

No. 27.—**World's Fair Buggy.** Price, $250 to $350.

This is a very elaborately finished article; carved body, beautifully ornamented; loops, braces, scrolls, rail, and back full plated; extra leather top; trimmed beautifully with any desired material; richly carved, and finished throughout with the very best materials.

No. 28.—**Gipsy No Top.** Price, $135 to $165.

A neat and pretty style, on suspension scroll loops. Iron dash, stirrup steps, creased leather boot, plated seat rail, and loops.

No. 29.—**Montgomery Top.** Price, $165 to $195.

Good style, plain, neat, and substantial; roomy, comfortable, and convenient. Shifting top, iron dash, branch steps, and in general appearance attractive.

No. 30.—**Florence No Top.** Price, $140 to $170.

A very fine and showy Buggy. Finished with full plated scroll loops; braces, steps, and back. Sides sometimes ornamented with silver ornaments. Is usually finished light. Altogether it is a very attractive Buggy.

No. 31.—**Imperial No Top.** Price, $155 to $185.

A very attractive and fine appearing Buggy. The irons being nearly all full plated, panels sometimes inlaid with pearl and silver, and every part of it being finished in a superior manner, makes it the most showy Buggy in use.

No. 32.—**Premium Top.** Price, $300 to $500.

The cut of this is very correct, fully showing the beautiful style and workmanship of the justly called Premium Buggy; to which the best of judges have assented. It is handsomely carved and painted, trimmed with velvet and silk, irons gracefully scrolled, and full plated. In short, it is the finest Buggy ever made.

No. 33.—**Mobile Top.** Price, $160 to $200.

A good style, usually finished plain. Straight body, leather dash, stick seat, shifting top, branch steps. Is well liked, and much in use in Southern cities.

No. 34.—**Skeleton Wagon.** Price, $80 to $95.

No. 35.—**Eureka Jump Seat.** Price, $250 to $325.

The most elegant of all shifting-seat Buggies. It is now shown as a graceful Phaeton, with high, easy back, and having every appearance of a single Buggy. By one motion it can be changed into a two-seat form, as shown in No. 35 B. Finished in the very best and most stylish manner. For certificates and recommendations, see page 32.

No. 35 B.—**Eureka Jump Seat.** Price, $250 to $325.

Same as No. 35.

No. 36.—**Antique No Top.** Price, $95 to $125.

Finished plain, crooked body, wood dash, solid seat, open back, iron rack, stirrup steps. Cheap, but good.

No. 37.—**Antique Top.** Price, $135 to $175.

Same style body as No. 36, with four bow shifting top, full plate joints, high back. Roomy and comfortable.

No. 38.—**Doctors' Phaeton.** Price, $225 to $260.

A style particularly adapted to the use of professional men. Crooked body, easy of access, high back, and very roomy. Close top, with back and side lights. Leather dash, large full apron, and solid steps. Made of the very best material, having no traps about it to rattle or get out of order.

No. 39.—**Park Phaeton.** Price, $225 to $265.

This style presents a very pleasing appearance, and is highly recommended. Is finished up fine and showy, full plated, finely painted and ornamented, and is a beautiful, easy, and comfortable Carriage.

No. 41.—**Victoria Buggy.** Price, $145 to $225.

With a beautifully carved and ornamented crooked body, wood dash, shifting top, full plated joints and braces, solid loop, ware iron and step, and iron rack. It presents a light and tasty appearance, and is much liked. Turns short, and is easy of access.

No. 42.—**Plantation No Top.** Price, $85 to $115.

Plain, low-priced Buggy. Roomy, strong, and convenient.

No. 43.—**Plantation Top.** Price, $130 to $165.

Same style as No. 42, with shifting top and high back. Good for service.

No. 44.—**Medium No Top.** Price, $95 to $125.

Good, cheap, and strong, and suitable for hard roads. Wood dash, stitched boot, and open back. Very comfortable.

No. 45.—**Medium Top.** Price, $135 to $175.

Same as No. 44, with shifting top.

No. 46.—**Cut Under No Top.** Price, $95 to $130.

Crooked body, neat box, wood dash, open back, stirrup steps, plated rail and braces. Turns short, and is easy to get in and out of.

No. 47.—**Farmers' Buggy.** Price, $140 to $175.

With crooked body and wood dash; four bow shifting top, high back, full plated joints and braces, box behind. Good style, and, for the price, very desirable.

No. 49.—**Cash Buggy.**   Price, $125 to $160.

Crooked body, leather dash, shifting top, high back, stirrup steps, full plated joints.   Best Buggy for the price now made. Gives general satisfaction.

No. 50.—**Student Buggy.**   Price, $135 to $165.

A very light and neat style, ornamented panels, carved bars, plated steps, and finished very tasty.   One of the latest styles out.

No. 51.—**Elm City Top.**   Price, $200 to $250.

A new and beautiful style, made of the best materials and work.   Plain, but neatly finished, with leather or prunelle top. Cut shows with Sarvin's patent wheel, a great improvement, and the best and strongest wheel in use.   The Elm City cannot fail to please those who want a good, light, and neat top Buggy.   The latest style out, and is really very fine.

No. 53.—**New Orleans Jump Seat.**   Price, $200 to $250.

Crooked body and wood dash, with same attachments as the Box Jump Seat.   Shifting top, high back, and full plated.   Is fine and elegant in appearance, and generally liked.   See recommendations and certificates, on page 32.

No. 53 B.—**New Orleans Jump Seat.**   Price, $200 to $250.

Same as No. 53.

No. 54.—**Jump Seat Barouche.**   Price, $225 to $275.

A new and desirable style of shifting seat extension top.   Front seat folds back and back seat jumps, as shown in No. 54 B.   Is comfortable, and convenient for two or four persons.   When in one seat form the top folds up, as shown in cut.   Can be changed in less than half a minute.

No. 54 B.—**Jump Seat Barouche.**   Price, $225 to $275.

Same as No. 54, in two seat form.

No. 55.—**Quinnipiack Jump Seat.**   Price, $225 to $275.

A beautiful light Rockaway, with the adjustable seats.   For a one-horse family vehicle this is very convenient.   Crooked body, leather dash, and high, comfortable backs; neatly finished; double steps.   A new style, very much admired for its comfort and convenience.

No. 55 B.—**Quinnipiack Jump Seat.**   Price, $225 to $275.

Same as No. 55, in two seat form.

No. 57.—**Cricket.**   Price, $120 to $160.

A very light no top, on side springs.   Straight body, iron dash, and light stick seat.   Is an admirable Buggy for trotting purposes. Fancy boot, ornamented, and plain trimming.   The lightest style in use; weighs from 160 to 225 pounds.

No. 58.—**Road Sulky.**   Price, $75 to $95.

No. 59.—**Whitney Wagon.**   Price, $175 to $210.

No. 60.—**Boston Chaise.**   Price, $200 to $250.

No. 61.—**Gazelle.**   Price, $150 to $180.

No. 62.—**Jagger.**   Price, $100 to $140.

No. 63.—**Prince of Wales.**   Price, $225 to $275.

No. 64.—**Champion.**   Price, $225 to $275.

Nos. 61, 63, and 64 are all new styles, and must be seen to be fully appreciated; but for style and finish they cannot be *beat*. Being finished with the best homogeneous steel axles and tire, tempered springs, &c., they are all of them very light and desirable.

No. 66.—**Dayton Brett.**   Price, $450 to $600.

No. 67.—**Child's Seat Drop Front.**   Price, $145 to $185.

No. 68.—**Crescent City.**   Price, $220 to $260.

No. 69.—**Full Top Cabriolet.**   Price, $300 to $350.

No. 70.—**Slide Seat Buggy.**   Price, $160 to $200.

No. 101.—**Gipsy Brett.**   Price, $325 to $450.

No. 102.—**Coupe Rockaway.**   Price, $325 to $450.

No. 103.—**C Spring Coach.**   Price, $450 to $700.

No. 104.—**Hamilton Coach.**   Price, $900 to $1,200.

No. 105.—**Family Coach.**   Price, $600 to $800.

No. 107.—**Lawrence Brett.**   Price, $700 to $950.

No. 108.—**Light Coupe.**   Price, $350 to $500.

No. 109.—**Crane Neck Coach.**   Price, $800 to $1,000.

No. 111.—**Livery Coach.**   Price, $450 to $650.

No. 112.—**Shifting Front Rockaway.**   Price, $325 to $400.

No. 113.—**Panel Quarter Rockaway.**   Price, $375 to $475.

No. 114.—**Jump Seat Top Wagon.**   Price, $150 to $200.

No. 115.—**Brewster Calash Coach.**   Price, $900 to $1,150.

No. 116.—**Full Scroll Brett.**   Price, $500 to $700.

No. 119.—**Carved Charriottee.**   Price, $275 to $325.

No. 120.—**Houston Rockaway.**   Price, $225 to $300.

No. 121.—**Light Calash Coach.**   Price, $850 to $1,000.

No. 122.—**Continental Rockaway.**   Price, $700 to $800.

No. 123.—**English Phaeton.**   Price, $450 to $650.

No. 124.—**French Dog Cart.**   Price, $400 to $600.

No. 125.—**Six Seat Germantown.** Price, $400 to $600.

No. 126.—**Yorktown Rockaway.** Price, $300 to $400.

No. 128.—**Loop Calash.** Price, $800 to $1,000.

No. 129.—**Full Size Calash.** Price, $700 to $900.

No. 130.—**City Coupe.** Price, $700 to $900.

No. 131.—**Four Seat Germantown.** Price, $220 to $275.

No. 132.—**Brougham Rockaway.** Price, $550 to $700.

No. 133.—**Six Seat Barouche.** Price, $400 to $475.

No. 134.—**Louisiana Rockaway.** Price, $400 to $550.

No. 135.—**New Haven Barouche.** Price, $350 to $400.

No. 136.—**Shifting Quarter Coach.** Price, $600 to $800.

No. 137.—**Alabama Six Seat.** Price, $300 to $375.

No. 138.—**Carved Turn Over Seat.** Price, $190 to $230.

No. 139.—**Light Open Five Seat.** Price, $270 to $320.

No. 140.—**Fine Shifting Quarter Rockaway.** $425 to $550.

No. 141.—**Light Four Seat Rockaway.** Price, $225 to $300.

No. 142.—**Turn Over Seat Rockaway.** Price, $170 to $230.

No. 143.—**Light Perch Coach.** Price, $600 to $775.

No. 145.—**New Orleans Charriottee.** Price, $310 to $400.

A definite description of the Coaches and Rockaways would be altogether fruitless, owing to the many different styles of trimming and finish. The cuts are very good representations of the vehicles themselves, and from which a good idea can be obtained.

INDEX TO ADVERTISEMENTS.

REMARKS.

WE have great satisfaction in introducing to our widely-scattered readers the houses whose business cards appear in this book. We have aimed to allow the privileges of an appearance here only to first class establishments, such as it will be a pleasure to deal with. We are personally acquainted with those in New Haven, and, indeed, with nearly every one in the book, and believe them to be reliable, honorable business houses.

A great variety of trades and employments is here represented, but, for the most part, only one of a kind, so that a really large part of the articles of extended commerce, and of the more important branches of industry, are duly set forth. We hope that this information will prove of wide advantage to all concerned—that it will lead to an extended commerce, and prove another inducement to traders, and those in need of the facilities and the products here advertised, to visit or correspond with those teeming hives of industry whose enterprise, genius, thrift, and perseverance in their thousand separate ways, are creating and diffusing so much wealth and working out so peacefully new means of blessing to mankind. We cannot speak for each, nor do we need to, for all have spoken for themselves.

G. & D. COOK & CO.

No. 1.

The Wide World.

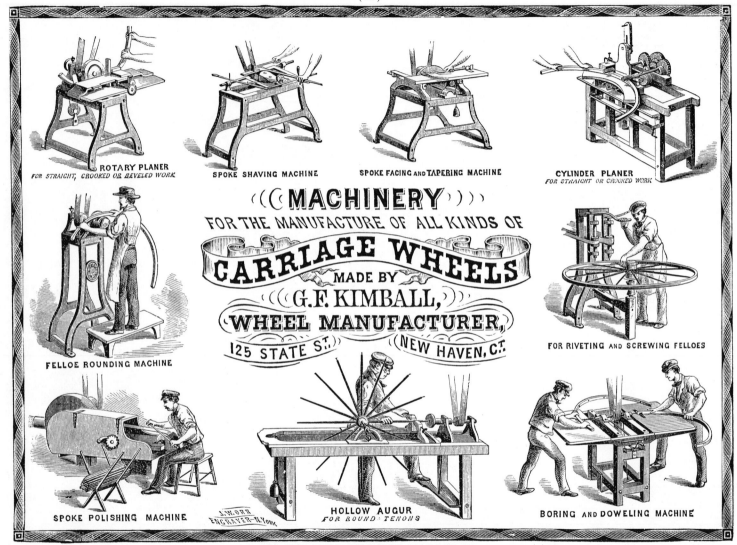

ROTARY PLANER
FOR STRAIGHT, CROOKED OR BEVELED WORK

SPOKE SHAVING MACHINE

SPOKE FACING AND TAPERING MACHINE

CYLINDER PLANER
FOR STRAIGHT OR CROOKED WORK

MACHINERY
FOR THE MANUFACTURE OF ALL KINDS OF
CARRIAGE WHEELS
MADE BY
G. F. KIMBALL,
WHEEL MANUFACTURER,
125 STATE ST., NEW HAVEN, C T.

FELLOE ROUNDING MACHINE

FOR RIVETING AND SCREWING FELLOES

SPOKE POLISHING MACHINE

J. W. ORR
ENGRAVER N. York

HOLLOW AUGUR
FOR ROUND TENONS

BORING AND DOWELING MACHINE

☞ SEE ADVERTISEMENT ON PAGE 128.

G. & D. COOK & CO.

No. 2.

LEGION.

P. JEWELL & SONS,

Manufacturers of

LEATHER BELTING

AND

LACE LEATHER,

220, 222, and 224 State Street,

HARTFORD, CONN.

No. 3.

THE GEM,

☞ SEE ADVERTISEMENT ON PAGE 104.

G. & D. COOK & CO.

No. 4.

PRIDE OF THE SOUTH.

RAYNOLDS, DEVOE & PRATT,

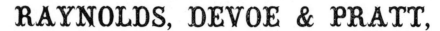

DEALERS IN PAINTS, OILS, &c.

106 & 108 Fulton Street, New York.

BLACKS.
Lamp Black, Super Velvet.
Drop   "   "   English.
Ivory   "   Genuine.

BLUES.
Ultramarine Blue, Extra Fine.
Chinese   "   "   "
Prussian   "   "   "

BROWNS.
Umbers and Siennas.
Purple Brown.
Vandyke "

GREENS.
Chrome Green, Extra Fine.
Quaker or Olive Green.
Bronze Green.

FILLING UP.
A Superior Article,
Packed in Boxes of 50 lbs.
  "   " Bbls. " 300 "

YELLOWS.
English Chrome Yellow, extra fine.
American "   "   pure.
English Dutch Pink.

REDS.
Vermilion, Engh. Pale and Deep.
Persian Red.
Indian "
Orange Mineral, best.

WHITES.
Genuine Engh. White Lead.
Cremnitz White.
Flake   "
Silver   "

CARMINES.
Carmine No. 40, Pure.
Carmine Lakes.
Crimson   "
Scarlet   "
Purple   "
Münich   "

BRUSHES.
Extra Ground Paint Brushes.
Flat Varnish Brushes, best French
    Bristles.
Fitch Hair Varnish Brushes.
Camel's Hair "   "
Badger Hair "   "

PENCILS.
Sable Hair Stripers and Writers.
Camel's "   "   "
Camel's " Swan Quill.

All Goods warranted of the best Quality.   For full particulars, send for Catalogue.

G. & D. COOK & CO.

No. 5.

Queen's Phaeton.

WHEELER & WILSON'S
SEWING MACHINES,

THE GREAT ECONOMIZER OF TIME AND PRESERVER OF HEALTH,

Have won the Highest Premiums at the Fair of the United States Agricultural Society ; at the State Fairs of Maine, Vermont, Connecticut, New York, New Jersey, Pennsylvania, Virginia, Mississippi, Missouri, Ohio, Indiana, Illinois, Kentucky, Michigan, Wisconsin, California, and at the Fairs of the American Institute, New York ; Mechanics' Association, Boston ; Franklin Institute, Philadelphia ; Mechanics' Institute, Baltimore ; Metropolitan Mechanics' Institute, Washington ; Mechanics' Association, Cincinnati ; Kentucky Institute, Louisville ; Mechanical Association, St. Louis ; Mechanics' Institute, San Francisco ; and at hundreds of County Fairs.

Office, 505 BROADWAY, N. Y.

The Lock Stitch made by this Machine is the only stitch that cannot be raveled, and that presents the same appearance each side of the seam. It is made with two threads, one upon each side of the fabric, and interlocked in the center of it.

—:o:—

ECONOMY OF SEWING MACHINES.

The Wheeler & Wilson Sewing Machine Company has prepared tables showing by actual experiment of four different workers the time required to stitch each part of a garment by hand, and with their Sewing Machine. The superiority of the work done by the Machine, and the healthfulness of the employment are advantages quite as great as the saving of time. Subjoined is a summary of several of the tables :—

	By Machine. Hours. Mins.	By Hand. Hours. Mins.		By Machine. Hours. Mins.	By Hand. Hours. Mins.
Gentlemen's Shirts..1	16	14 26	Calico Dress.........	57	6 37
Frock Coats.........2	38	16 35	Chemise 1	1	10 31
Satin Vests.........1	14	7 19	Moreen Skirt........	35	7 28
Linen "	48	5 14	Muslin "	30	6 1
Cloth Pants.........	51	5 10	Night Dress.........1	7	10 2
Summer "	38	2 50	Drawers	28	5 6
Silk Dress...........1	13	10 22	Silk Apron...........	15	4 16
Merino Dress.......1	4	8 27	Plain "	9	1 26

Seams of any considerable length are stitched, ordinarily, at the rate of a yard a minute.

Sewing Machine Awards by the American Institute, N. Y.

Sewing Machines, considered in their social, industrial, and physiological bearings upon society, are second in importance to no material agent of the day. Economizing nine-tenths of the time required for sewing by hand; eliminating most of the evils of needlework; enlarging the sphere of woman's employment by creating new and profitable branches of industry; relieving the housekeeper of her most grievous burden, the Sewing Machines rank with the fabled deities as benefactors of humanity.

The Committee of the American Institute, N. Y., appointed at the late exhibition at Palace Garden to examine Sewing Machines, have made a long, elaborate, and able report, of much interest to the public. Although the utility of this invention is established beyond all question, yet, for the various purposes of its application, ignorance exists as to the particular patent best for a specific purpose. Committees heretofore have not discriminated and classified sufficiently. This report is free from these faults. The Machines are arranged according to the stitch made and the purpose to which the machine is to be applied, in four classes, 1st, 2d, 3d, and 4th; a classification indicating the general order of merit and importance:

CLASS 1ST includes the Shuttle or Lock Stitch Machines for family use, and for manufacturers in the same range of purpose and material. The Committee has assigned this class the highest rank, on account of the "elasticity, permanence, beauty, and general desirableness of the stitching when done," and the wide range of its application. At the head of this class they place the Wheeler & Wilson Machine, and award it the highest premium. This has been the uniform award for this Machine throughout the country for several years, and we think no disinterested person will dispute its justice and propriety.

CLASS 2D includes the Shuttle or Lock Stitch Machines for heavy manufacturing purposes. At the head of this class the Committee places First & Frost's Machines.

CLASS 3D includes the Double Chain Stitch Machines. The Grover & Baker Machine is placed at the head of this class. The Committee objects to the stitch made by this Machine, inasmuch as it consumes more thread than any other stitch, and leaves a ridge projecting from one side of the seam. This, in the Committee's opinion, must usually impair the durability of the seam, and often the beauty of the garments or other articles so stitched, though some of the Machines making this stitch can be used very successfully for embroidering purposes.

CLASS 4TH includes the Single Thread Tambour or Chain Stitch Machines. The tendency of this stitch to ravel, the Committee considers an objection so serious that they refuse to recommend the Machines making it for any premium.

The public is much indebted to this Committee for the able discharge of their duty, in rendering clear a subject that interest has so much darkened.

WHEELER & WILSON'S SEWING MACHINES.

NEW STYLE MACHINE, $50.
HEMMER, IN ALL CASES, EXTRA, $5.

MEDIUM, ON PLAIN TABLE, $75.

MEDIUM, IN HALF CASE, PANELED, $80;
MAHOGANY, OR BLACK WALNUT VARNISHED, $85.

MEDIUM, IN FULL CASE, MAHOGANY OR
BLACK WALNUT, $100; ROSEWOOD, $115.

THE WHEELER & WILSON MANUFACTURING CO.

Invites the attention of Housekeepers, Seamstresses, Dressmakers, Tailors, Manufacturers of Shirts, Collars, Skirts, Cloaks, Mantillas, Clothing, Hats, Caps, Corsets, Ladies' Gaiters, Linen Goods, Umbrellas, Parasols and Silk Goods, to the perfect adaptation and unrivaled excellence of these SEWING MACHINES for their uses. Their extensive and increasing sale, and the unanimous commendation that they have received, warrant the Company in warmly recommending them. They have been in use sufficiently long to test them thoroughly, and have given entire satisfaction.

They are simple in construction, efficient and durable in operation, beautiful in model and finish, fitted to adorn the parlor, and suited to the workshop—applicable alike to the use of the family and the manufacturer. Their speed is from 1,200 to 2,000 stitches per minute, or equal in efficiency to 12 seamstresses. Substituting, as they do, healthful exercises and rational employment for the soul-and-body-destroying drudgery of hand-sewing, they are hailed as WOMAN'S FRIEND.

Among their undoubted advantages are—

1. Elegance of model and finish; 2. Simplicity and thoroughness of construction, and consequent durability and freedom from derangement and need of repairs; 3. Ease of management, and rapidity and quietness of operation; 4. Hemming and seaming attachments; 5. Beauty of Stitch, alike on both sides of the fabric sewed; 6. Strength and firmness of seam, that will not rip nor ravel; and made with 7. Economy of Thread; 8. Applicability to a variety of purposes and materials.

The change made in the tension during the past year, so that the upper thread is used from the original spool, and the addition of the hemmer, by which hems of any width are turned and stitched without any previous basting, evince the care of the Company in incorporating with the machines every device that can tend to perfecting them. They now combine every improvement that has been invented for sewing, and the Company feels confident that, in their present form, they are by far the best ever offered to the public; and refers, for confirmation of this opinion, to the thousands of families and manufacturers who use them.

G. & D. COOK & CO.

No. 6.

BOX JUMP SEAT.

G.&D. COOK & CO.

No. 6 B.

BOX JUMP SEAT.

James Punderford.   Jas. A. Punderford.

NEW HAVEN, CONNECTICUT.

J. PUNDERFORD & SON,

TANNERS, CURRIERS,

AND WHOLESALE DEALERS IN

Hides, Leather, Oil,

AND

SHOE FINDINGS,

French, German & American

CALF SKINS,

PATENT

AND

Enameled Leather,

MOROCCO, &c.

Constantly on hand, of our own
Manufacture,

*Oak Sole, Harness, Bridle, Grain,
and Wax Leather.*

MANUFACTURERS

AND

Wholesale Dealers

IN

Boots and Shoes

OF ALL KINDS,

Adapted to the Trade of
Every Section of the Country.

PARTICULAR ATTENTION

GIVEN TO THE MANUFACTURE OF

Gem's Fine Calf

SEWED & PEGGED BOOTS,

Oxford Ties,

*Strap Pumps, English Lace Boots,
Balmorals, Congress Boots, &c.*

ALSO,

Ladies' Fine Sewed Work

IN GREAT VARIETY.

103, 105 & 107 George Street, New Haven, Conn.

BOOTS, SHOES, AND LEATHER.

The proprietors of this concern have been engaged in this business, in this City, for more than **Thirty Years**, and possessing **every facility** to conduct the manufacture of our Goods on **extensive** and **systematic** principles, we solicit the patronage of **the trade**, at home and abroad, especially those who prefer to obtain Goods **direct from the Manufacturer**, without paying an **additional profit.**

We pledge ourselves to fill orders by mail with **promptness** and **fidelity** to the interests of the purchaser, and, relying upon a reputation which it has been our aim so many years to establish, we respectfully solicit the favors of correspondents.   **J. P. & SON.**

No. 7.

PHILADELPHIA TOP.

COOK'S ADJUSTABLE CARRIAGE SEATS.

THIS arrangement for adjusting Carriage Seats was Patented by GEORGE & DAVID COOK, of New Haven, Conn., February 3d, 1857.

They are adapted to almost any style of Carriage—can be used on a crooked as well as a straight body—and are at present being used extensively throughout the New England States, on light Rockaways as well as all styles of Open and Top Buggies. The peculiar merits and advantages of this invention over the ordinary sliding-seat, or in fact any other mode of adjustment, consists,

1st. That the seats are perfectly secure and firm in either form, without the use of thumb-screws or bolts.

2d. They can be changed from a one to a two-seat carriage, and *vice versa*, by any person, in less than five seconds.

3d. Their construction is such there is no possibility of RATTLING.

4th. They are so simple in their construction that they do not get out of repair.

5th. The perfect symmetry of the Carriage is preserved in either form, so that, when in one-seat form, no one unacquainted with them would ever think there was another seat concealed.

6th. The manner in which they *jump* instead of sliding, is such, that in changing them the paint is not marred or scratched. In short, the simplicity, ease of construction, durability, and lightness, together with the most perfect principle heretofore introduced, must necessarily commend itself to Carriage Makers generally, and at once take the precedence of all other modes of adjusting seats now in use.

CERTIFICATES.

We, the undersigned, Carriage Makers of New Haven, Conn., have examined, and seen in operation, the past two years, G. & D. COOK's PATENT ADJUSTABLE CARRIAGE SEATS, and can recommend them to manufacturers and dealers with the highest degree of confidence as an article combining every desired quality requisite in a *shifting seat*, and decidedly the best arrangement we have ever seen.

We fully concur in all the Messrs. Cook's claim " in detail" for it in their circular of March 1st, 1859.

LAWRENCE, BRADLEY & PARDEE, *New Haven, Ct.*
W. & C. DICKERMAN,   "   "   "
H. HOOKER & CO.,   "   "   "
OSBORN & ADRIANCE,   "   "   "

G. & D. COOK & CO.

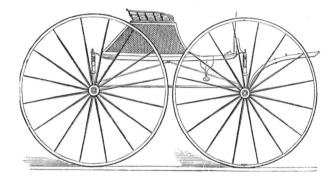

No. 10.

JOCELYN NO TOP.

WOODRUFF & BEACH IRON WORKS, HARTFORD, CONN.

HIGH AND LOW PRESSURE

MARINE AND STATIONARY STEAM ENGINES,

STEAM BOILERS, AND ALL KINDS OF MACHINERY, MADE TO ORDER.

BUILDERS OF THE PUMPING ENGINES IN THE CITIES OF Brooklyn, N. Y., and Hartford, Conn.

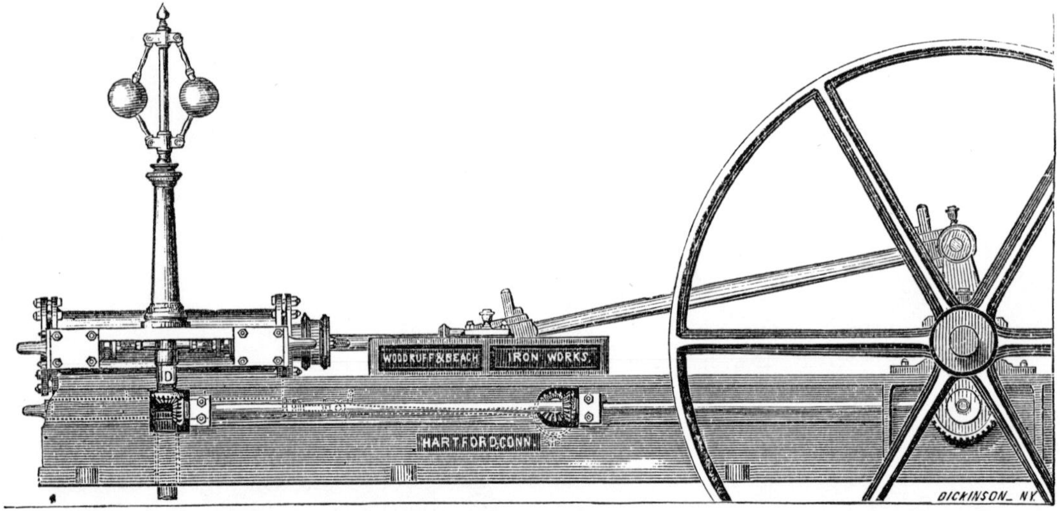

BUILDERS OF THE Steam Machinery of the U. S. Screw Propeller SLOOP-OF-WAR MOHICAN.

WOODRUFF & BEACH IRON WORKS

HARTFORD, CONN.

DICKINSON. NY

We would particularly invite the notice of the public to our Patent "Self Adjusting Cut Off," which, after a thorough practical test of several years, is universally acknowledged to possess more advantages than any other in use. Its principle and construction is entirely original, and has the merit of remarkable simplicity, combined with durability of workmanship. Its application is direct, easily kept in order, and seldom needs repair—certainly not more than once in five years. It is the cheapest and best, and produces higher economical results than any other in existence. We feel confident that it will fully meet the expectations of our customers, and do all, if not more, than we claim for it.

SAMUEL WOODRUFF, Pres't.   **T. S. ROOT, Sec'y.**   **H. B. BEACH, Treas.**   **WILLIAM WRIGHT, Eng'r.**

No. 11.

PHILADELPHIA NO TOP.

MANUFACTURERS

OF

WHEELS

AND

Wheel Stuffs

Of every description,

Spokes,

HUBS,

RIMS,

Sawed Felloes

SPRING BARS,

Plain and Carved,

Whiffletrees,

SEAT STICKS,

&c.,

On hand and made to order, of the best of Eastern Timber.

NEW HAVEN, CONN.

Also, Manufacturers of

SARVEN'S PATENT WHEEL,

Which, for lightness and durability, excel all other Wheels made.

NEW HAVEN, *May 16th,* 1860.

I, James D. Sarven, hereby certify that the NEW HAVEN WHEEL CO., per HENRY G. LEWIS, *Secretary,* and Messrs. WOODBURN & SCOTT, of St. Louis, Mo., have the exclusive right to manufacture my PATENT WHEEL, and sell the same as an article of merchandise to those not owning shop rights.   JAMES D. SARVEN.

For particulars in regard to the PATENT WHEEL, or shop rights, address either of the parties.

HENRY G. LEWIS, Secretary.

GIPSY TOP.

DOREMUS & NIXON,

IMPORTERS OF AND DEALERS IN

FURNISHING DRY GOODS,

21 Park Place and 18 Murray Street, New York,

HAVE CONSTANTLY ON HAND EVERY DESCRIPTION OF DRY GOODS REQUIRED

For Ships, Hotels, Public Institutions, and Private Dwellings,

SUCH AS OIL CLOTHS, CARPETS, DRUGGETS, COCOA AND CHINA MATTING,
BLANKETS, COUNTERPANES, QUILTS, DAMASK LINENS, EVERY VARIETY, COTTON SHEETINGS, ALL WIDTHS, &c., &c.

ALSO,

For Car, Omnibus, and Carriage Manufacturers, Upholsterers, and Cabinet-Makers,

AMONG WHICH ARE PLUSHES, MOQUETTES, CANVAS FOR CAR ROOFING, COTELINES, SILKS, BROCATELLES, REPS,
WOOLEN CLOTHS, ENAMELED CLOTHS, DAMASKS, LASTINGS, &c., &c.,

WITH EVERY VARIETY OF TRIMMINGS SUITED TO THE TRADE.

ALSO,

FOR CHURCHES,

DAMASKS, MOREENS, AND GERMAN REPS FOR CUSHIONS.
MOHAIR PLUSH AND SILK VELVET FOR PULPIT CUSHIONS.
CARPETINGS, CHURCH PATTERNS AND COLORS.

COCOA MATTINGS AND MATS.
COMMUNION DAMASK AND NAPKINS.
CURLED HAIR, in Rope, Picked, or made in Cushions.

MOSS BY THE BALE.

Merchants and Manufacturers are invited to call and examine our Stock.

G. & D. COOK & CO.

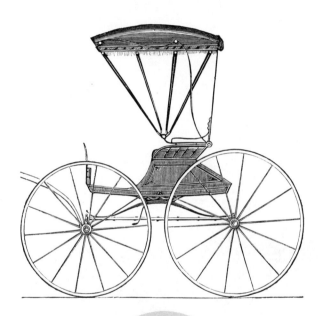

No. 15.

CONCORD TOP.

NETTLETON & ROWAN,
ATTORNEYS AND COUNSELORS AT LAW,

111 BROADWAY,

(Trinity Building, First Floor, Room No. 7,)

CHARLES NETTLETON, }
D. NOBLE ROWAN. }

NEW YORK.

Mr. ROWAN REFERS TO

Hon. JOHN W. EDMONDS, New York City.	Hon. HORATIO SEYMOUR, Utica, N. Y.
" GILBERT DEAN, " " "	" ROSCOE CONKLING, " "
JAMES T. BRADY, Esq., " " "	" CHAS. H. RUGGLES, Po'keepsie
CLAFLIN, MELLEN & CO. " " "	" HENRY BOOTH, Sen., Professor Law
Hon. JOHN KELLY, Sheriff of City and County	School, Chicago, Ill.
of New York.	

CHARLES NETTLETON,
NOTARY PUBLIC AND COMMISSIONER
FOR

Maine, New Hampshire, Vermont, Rhode Island, Massachusetts, Connecticut, New York, New Jersey, Pennsylvania, Maryland, Virginia, North Carolina, South Carolina, Georgia, Alabama, Mississippi, Louisiana, Tennessee, Kentucky, Ohio, Indiana, Illinois, Michigan, Wisconsin, Minnesota, Iowa, Missouri, Kansas, Arkansas, Texas, California, Oregon, and Washington Territory.

The undersigned, members of the Legal Profession, practicing in the City of New York, take pleasure in recommending to the Public generally, and especially to the members of the Bar, CHAS. NETTLETON, Esq., as a suitable person to take Depositions to be used in the Courts of the United States, and of the several States of the Union. In addition to personal integrity and varied experience in this line of practice, Mr. Nettleton has the Statute Laws of the several States as a guide.
NEW YORK, March 1st, 1859.

WM. CURTIS NOYES,	DAVID DUDLEY FIELD,	CHARLES O'CONOR,
FRANCIS B. CUTTING,	JAMES S. SLUYTER,	JAMES T. BRADY,
WM. M. EVARTS,	DUDLEY FIELD,	WILLIAM FULLERTON,
EDGAR S. VAN WINKLE,	HENRY J. SCUDDER,	BENJAMIN DUNNING,
THOMAS J. POWERS,	HENRY DAY,	WEEKS & DE FOREST.

Will pay special attention to the taking of DEPOSITIONS for the several State and United States Courts of the Union; and also to the DRAWING and ACKNOWLEDGMENT of DEEDS for the several States. Blank Deeds from the several States.

HAS THE STATUTES OF THE SEVERAL STATES.

LAW BOOKS.

By special arrangement with the Law Book Publishers of this City, Boston, and Philadelphia, I have facilities for the purchase of Elementary Law Books, and the Reports of the United States, the several State Courts, and the English Reports, at cheaper rates than are usually paid by the profession. I will execute orders for the purchase of all kinds of LAW BOOKS, from a single book to a library, and will price any list of Elementary Works or Reports sent me (with return postage stamp enclosed) by any member of the profession wishing to purchase the same.

My charge will be a commission of five per cent. on the amount purchased.

CHARLES NETTLETON,
Commissioner for the several States,
111 Broadway, New York.

G. & D. COOK & CO.

No. 16.

Georgia No Top.

ROBERT B. BRADLEY & CO.
FARMING TOOLS & MACHINES.

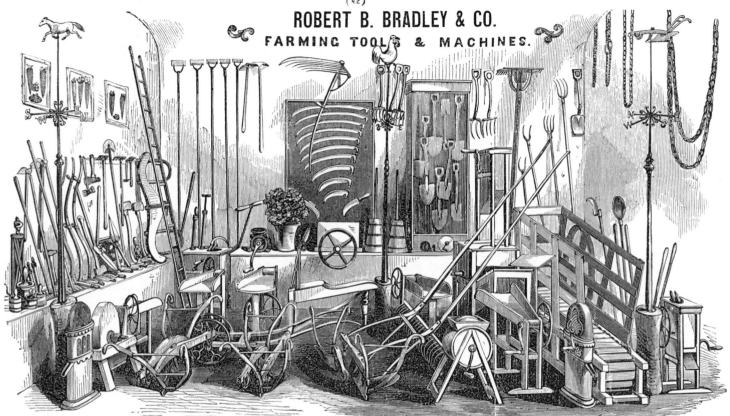

NEW HAVEN AGRICULTURAL WAREHOUSE AND SEED STORE,
93 STATE STREET, NEW HAVEN, CONN.
ROBERT B. BRADLEY & CO.,

Wholesale and Retail Dealers in Agricultural Machines and Implements of the most approved kinds, and Woodenware; Field, Grass, and Garden Seeds: Fertilizers—Peruvian and Fish Guano, Phosphate of Lime, Poudrette, Bone Dust, Gypsum, &c. Also, Manufacturers of Churns, Cultivators, Corn-Shellers, Fanning Mills, Hay or Feed Cutters, Store Trucks, &c., &c.

Farmers, Planters, and Dealers, wishing our circular and price list, will be furnished by sending us their address.

G. & D. COOK & CO.

No. 18.

CONCORD NO TOP.

H. H. SNOW,

Manufacturer and Dealer in

Pure American & French Confectionery

176 CHAPEL STREET, NEW HAVEN, Conn.

Dealers in any part of the Country supplied in quantities to suit at short notice.

CIRCULARS SENT TO ALL WHO MAY DESIRE THEM.

READER! DO YOU USE CONFECTIONERY?

Do you occasionally take a package HOME? If so, did you ever feel that you might be offering that which was not perfectly PURE?—something that possibly might injure those who are dear to you? If you have not, there are many who have experienced this doubt, and probably in many cases there has been sufficient cause. **SNOW has had more than 20 years' experience** (practically) in manufacturing first-class Confectionery, and for ten years past has been, and now is, doing business at 176 CHAPEL STREET, NEW HAVEN, where he has one of the most complete Manufactories in the country. For the benefit of his friends and customers, he has opened a fine store at **407 BROADWAY, New York,** and supplies it daily with

MORE THAN ONE HUNDRED KINDS OF

AMERICAN AND FRENCH CONFECTIONERY,

AS "PURE AS THE DEW-DROP."

G. & D. COOK & CO.

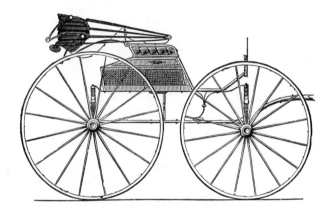

No. 19.

CANE SIDE BUGGY.

G. & D. COOK & CO.

No. 21.

CITY NO TOP.

IRON WAREHOUSE,

93 and 95 BARCLAY STREET, NEW YORK.

H. & J. HOPKINS

HAVE IN STORE A WELL-ASSORTED STOCK OF

IRON AND STEEL,

WHICH THEY OFFER, IN LOTS TO SUIT PURCHASERS, AT THE LOWEST PRICES.

Bagnal's, B B H, and American Charcoal Iron.
Common English Bar and Bolt Iron.
Norway, Swedes, and American Hammered Iron.
Horse Nail Rods, of T V F and U B brands.
Horse Shoe Iron, Slit, B B H, Peru, and Fall River brands.
Band, Hoop, Scroll, Oval, and Half-round Iron.
Steel—Spring, Toe-Cork, Tire and Sleigh Shoe; Norton's.
Steel—Cast, Shear, Blister (L), and German.

Residence of JOSEPH E. SHEFFIELD, N.H. Conn.

Engraved on Wood by J. W. Orr N.Y.

HENRY AUSTIN,   **ARCHITECT,**
Office, Street's Building, Chapel St.
New Haven, Conn.

G. & D. COOK & CO.

No. 22.

Sporting Wagon.

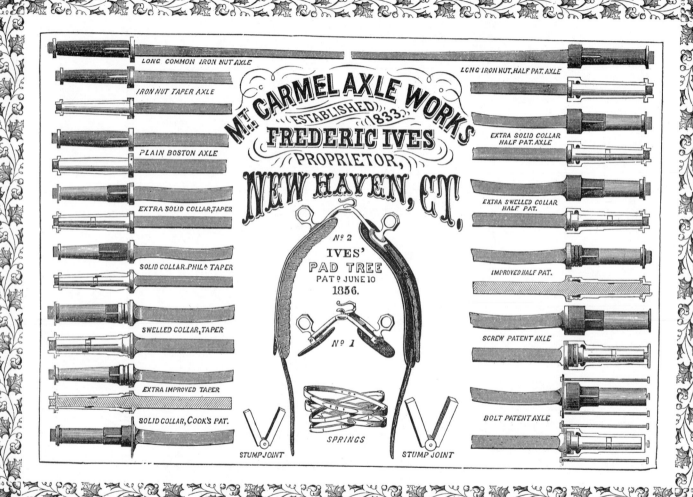

LONG COMMON IRON NUT AXLE

IRON NUT TAPER AXLE

PLAIN BOSTON AXLE

EXTRA SOLID COLLAR, TAPER

SOLID COLLAR, PHILa TAPER

SWELLED COLLAR, TAPER

EXTRA IMPROVED TAPER

SOLID COLLAR, COOK'S PAT.

MT CARMEL AXLE WORKS
ESTABLISHED 1833
FREDERIC IVES
PROPRIETOR,
NEW HAVEN, CT.

Nº 2
IVES'
PAD TREE
PATd JUNE 10
1856.

Nº 1

STUMP JOINT

SPRINGS

STUMP JOINT

LONG IRON NUT, HALF PAT. AXLE

EXTRA SOLID COLLAR
HALF PAT. AXLE

EXTRA SWELLED COLLAR
HALF PAT.

IMPROVED HALF PAT.

SCREW PATENT AXLE

BOLT PATENT AXLE

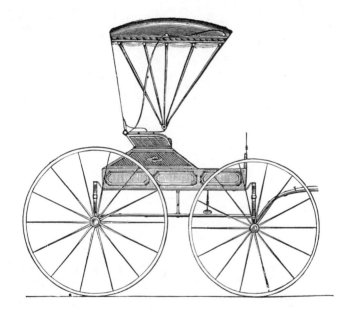

No. 23.

CITY TOP.

HENRY N. WHITTELSEY & CO.,

IMPORTERS AND DEALERS IN

CROCKERY, CHINA & GLASSWARE

OF EVERY DESCRIPTION,

ALSO,

FANCY GOODS,

93 CHAPEL STREET,   **NEW HAVEN, CONN.**

A Complete Assortment always on hand, suitable for Country trade. Orders solicited and Goods packed with care.

No. 24.

TONTINE TOP.

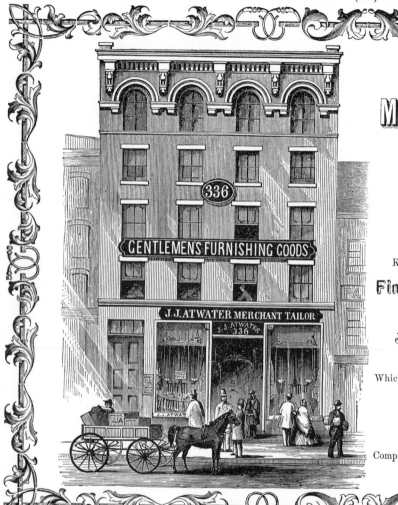

J. J. ATWATER,

MERCHANT TAILOR,

AND DEALER IN

GENTLEMEN'S FURNISHING GOODS,

No 336 CHAPEL STREET,

NEW HAVEN, CT.,

Keeps constantly on hand the best assortment in the city of

Fine Goods for Gentlemen's Wear,

FINE CLOTHS,

French and English Cassimeres,

WAISTCOATINGS of every variety,

Which will be made to order in the best manner, and in style not
to be excelled.

Furnishing Goods,

Comprising every article necessary to complete a GENTLEMAN'S
WARDROBE, and all NOVELTIES in that line.

G. & D. COOK & CO.

No. 25.

EXCELSIOR TOP.

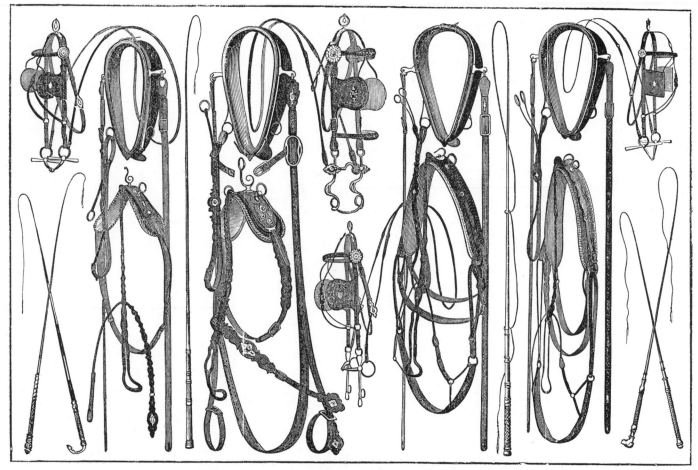

E. D. ATWATTER,
MANUFACTURER OF ALL STYLES OF HARNESS,
COR. STATE AND WALL STS. (near Cook's Factory), NEW HAVEN, CT.

G. & D. COOK & CO.

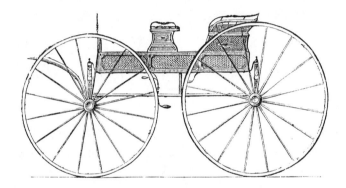

No. 26.

FRENCH JUMP SEAT.

JOHN W. ORR,

DESIGNER and ENGRAVER on WOOD,

ILLUSTRATED-CATALOGUE AND

ORNAMENTAL SHOW-CARD PRINTER,

ELECTROTYPER AND STEREOTYPER,

INVENTOR AND MANUFACTURER OF ILLUMINATED ENVELOPES, (Patent applied for,)

Nos. 75 and 77 NASSAU STREET, NEW YORK CITY.

The subscriber, having the largest and most complete Establishment of the kind in America, is fully prepared to execute all orders in his line, however large, in a superior style, with dispatch, and at reasonable prices. Particular attention paid to

DRAWING AND ENGRAVING ALL KINDS OF

Book Illustrations, Cuts for Illustrated Catalogues, Stoves, Machinery, Landscapes, Carriages, Cuts for Newspapers, Portraits of Men and of Animals, Views of Public Buildings, Large or Small Show Cards, (Plain or in Colors,) &c.

Superior Draughtsmen permanently engaged in the Establishment, who are always ready to go to any part of the United States or Canadas to make Drawings of Machinery, Buildings, &c. At this Establishment any article requiring the greatest possible accuracy of detail in its representation, such as

MACHINERY OF ANY KIND, PORTRAITS, &c.,

can be Photographed directly on the surface of the Wood, thus preventing any delay from the tedious method of drawing by hand. As the importance of this invention can only be understood or appreciated by those who have witnessed its wonderful results, the public are invited to call and examine Specimens. Orders by Mail, Express, or Telegraph, promptly attended to.

J. W. ORR,

No. 75 Nassau Street, New York City.

 For Specimens of some of the kinds of work done in this Establishment the public is referred to the Engravings in this Book

G. & D. COOK & CO.

No. 27.

World's Fair Buggy.

G. A. SHUBERT, STONE-CUTTER,

63 GRAND STREET, New Haven, Conn.

Orders for Buildings, Monuments, Posts, or any Stone Work, plain or ornamental, executed in Brown Stone or Granite, at the shortest notice.

The New Haven Custom House, Young Men's Institute, and Bank Building are a few of the many buildings I have executed.

Reference:—HENRY AUSTIN, SIDNEY M. STONE, Architect, New Haven, Conn.

G. & D. COOK & CO.

No. 28.

GIPSY NO TOP.

J. N. COLLINS.   P. S. CROFUT.

COLLINS & CO., Hatters and Furriers, No. 273 Chapel St., Old No. 111.

ESTABLISHED IN 1839.

Manufacturers, Jobbers, and Retail Dealers in all kinds of Dress Hats, Caps, French and American Soft Hats, Children's Fancy Hats and Caps, Traveling Trunks, Hat Cases, Valises, and Bags.

STRAW GOODS, Wholesale and Retail, AT LESS THAN NEW YORK PRICES.

LADIES' FANCY DRESS FURS.

Buffalo and Fancy Robes, the Best and Cheapest in the United States.   Dealers supplied.   Gents' Furnishing Goods at one half the usual cost.   Horse Blankets, Fur Over Shoes, &c., &c.

THE SECRET OF SUCCESSFUL BUSINESS IS GOOD GOODS, LOW PRICES, QUICK SALES, AND READY PAY.

COLLINS & CO., Introducers of Lowest Prices.

Orders by mail promptly executed.   Raw Furs bought.

G. & D. COOK & CO.

No. 29.

MONTGOMERY TOP.

G. & D. COOK & CO.'S

GENERAL

Shipping and Forwarding Agency,

NEW YORK.

Office, 83 SOUTH STREET.

Goods sent to us from any part of the country will be handled with care and forwarded with dispatch.

G. & D. COOK & CO.

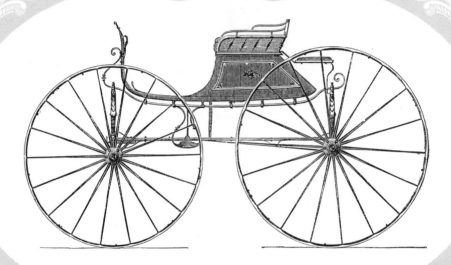

No. 30.

FLORENCE NO TOP.

E. B. & E. C. KELLOGG,

LITHOGRAPHERS,

No. 245 Main St., Hartford, Conn.,

(ESTABLISHED IN 1830,)

EXECUTE

PORTRAITS, LANDSCAPES,

Anatomical, Botanical, Architectural and Mechanical Drawings;

CIRCULARS, NOTES, DRAFTS, CHECKS, STOCK CERTIFICATES, BILL AND LETTER HEADS,

DRUGGISTS' AND MANUFACTURERS' LABELS,

SHOW CARDS FOR INSURANCE AND OTHER PURPOSES,

Views of Public Buildings, Private Residences, &c., &c., and all other work usually done in a well-furnished Establishment.

Publishers of Bougery & Jacobs' Elementary Anatomy, in Twenty Plates, one half the size of life; Redfield's Zoological Science; Redfield's Chart of the Animal Kingdom, together with a large assortment of Lithographic Prints, containing over six hundred different kinds. ALL ORDERS PROMPTLY ATTENDED TO.

G. & D. COOK & CO.

No. 31.

IMPERIAL NO TOP.

SAMUEL B. SMITH,

IMPORTER AND DEALER IN

Hardware, Cutlery, Iron and Steel,

FARMING UTENSILS,

BUILDERS' AND CABINET GOODS;

A LARGE ASSORTMENT OF

CARRIAGE GOODS,

Comprising in part the following, viz.:

AXLES,	BORAX, FILES,	LEATHER,	SHAFTS,
SPRINGS,	EMERY,	SCREWS,	POLES,
ANVILS,	GLUE,	BANDS,	SEATS,
VICES,	SAND PAPER,	PHIL'D BOLTS,	CARRIAGE PARTS,
SMITH BELLOWS,	ENAMELED CLOTH,		&c., &c., &c.

MECHANICS' TOOLS OF ALL KINDS.

238 Chapel Street,   New Haven, Conn.

G. & D. COOK & CO.

No. 32.

PREMIUM TOP.

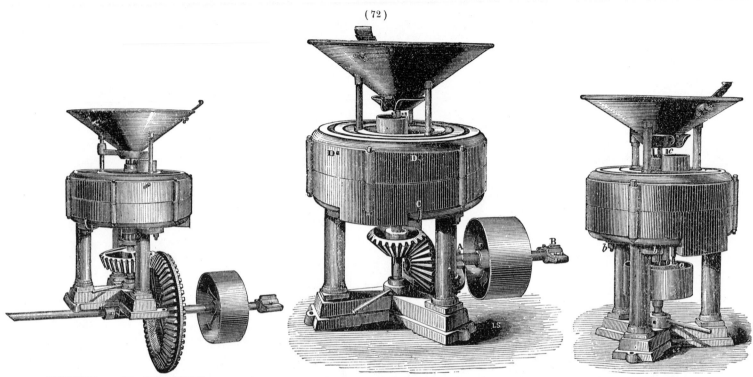

FLOUR AND GRAIN MILLS,

ADOPTED IN THE BEST MILLING ESTABLISHMENTS.

ALSO, SEVERAL VARIETIES FOR WET AND DRY PAINTS.

The first were patented and introduced in eighteen hundred and forty-seven. Afterward others, secured to me by letters patent, went rapidly into use, and about two thousand were put in operation. The important improvements in eighteen hundred and fifty-eight, together with the new devices lately adopted in their construction, produce a working capacity *never before known*. Three thousand have been sold already, and I am now constructing more than *thirty varieties*, so that they may be driven by any of the various applications of belts and gearing that may be required for all locations. To supply the increasing demand, my new building is now entirely occupied for manufacturing these Patent Burr Stone Mills. A new and enlarged edition of my illustrated mill circular, of one hundred pages, is now issuing from the press, with 20,000 copies for distribution, giving full particulars concerning my mills.

New Haven, Conn., June, 1860.

EDWARD HARRISON, No. 128 Orange Street.

G. & D. COOK & CO.

No. 33.

MOBILE TOP.

City Fire Insurance Company,

OF NEW HAVEN, CONN.

OFFICE, No. 84 CHAPEL STREET,

(BOARDMAN'S BUILDING.)

CHARTERED CAPITAL, . . . $500,000.
PAID UP CAPITAL AND SURPLUS, $320,653.

This Company insures BUILDINGS, MERCHANDISE, and PERSONAL PROPERTY on as favorable terms as other sound and well-conducted companies. Losses equitably adjusted and promptly paid. No losses have ever been litigated by this Company.

WELLS SOUTHWORTH, Pres.   **LEVI B. BRADLEY, Sec.**

DIRECTORS.

WM. W. BOARDMAN,	New Haven.	JAMES F. BABCOCK,	New Haven.	RUEL ROWE,	Fair Haven.
WM. JOHNSON,	"	JOSEPH E. SHEFFIELD,	"	HENRY L. CANNON,	New Haven.
NATH. R. DARRELL,	"	J. B. CARRINGTON,	"	NELSON HOTCHKISS,	"
MORRIS TYLER,	"	BENJ. NOYES,	"	E. SOUTHWORTH,	W. Springfield, Mass.
SMITH MERWIN,	"	GEORGE B. RICH,	"	JULIUS DAY,	" "
N. B. IVES,	"	WELLS SOUTHWORTH,	"	ELIHU ADAMS,	Springfield, Mass.
JAMES PUNDERFORD,	"	S. W. KNEVALS,	"	AARON BAGG,	W. Springfield, Mass.
THOMAS R. TROWBRIDGE,	"	E. C. SCRANTON,	"	L. BOLTWOOD,	Amherst, Mass.
SAMUEL NOYES,	"	M. G. ELLIOTT,	"	G. A. SMITH,	South Hadley, Mass.
AMBROSE TODD,	"	M. A. OSBORN,	"	J. H. SOUTHWORTH,	Philadelphia.
HENRY HALE	"	L. D. OLMSTED,	Chicago, Ill.	WILLIAM MATHER,	Simsbury, Conn.

G. & D. COOK & CO.

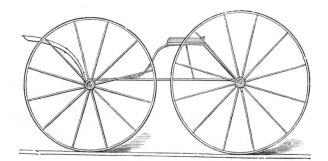

No. 34.

SKELETON WAGON.

TONTINE HOTEL, NEW HAVEN, CONNECTICUT.

The subscriber has refurnished this fashionable first-class Hotel entire this Spring, remodeled the old Dining Room, added a new Ladies' Ordinary, and put in complete order his Billiard and Bath Rooms. Families can have suites of rooms at either House as low as at any first-class House in the Country. Boarders can go to and from the TONTINE to the HEAD, three times a day, by rail, and take their meals at either House, without extra charge. Having purchased and stocked a large Farm at Sachem's Head this Spring, the two Houses will be furnished with Meats, Poultry, Milk, Butter, Vegetables, and Fruit, daily, from the Farm. A Telegraph line has been put up at Sachem's Head and at the Tontine, at the Proprietor's own expense, which connects with all the lines in the United States.

MAY 23, 1860.

H. LEE SCRANTON.

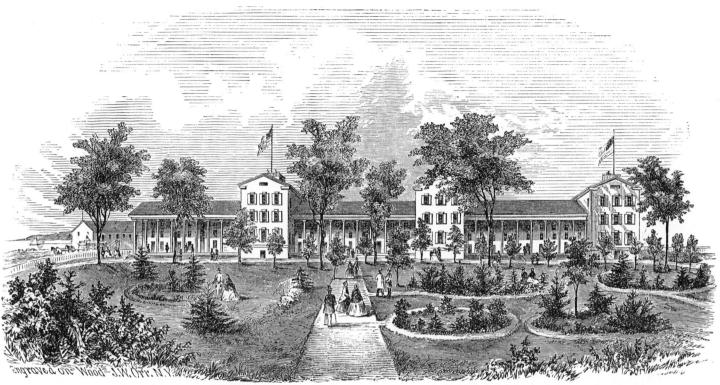

SACHEM'S HEAD HOTEL, GUILFORD, CONN.

The proprietor of this well-known first-class fashionable Summer-House would inform its former patrons and the public generally that he has built on three hundred feet this Spring, making seventy-four new bed rooms, new dining room forty by one hundred, new parlor forty by seventy. Every room in the house is newly furnished with *new Carpets* and new Cottage Furniture. The Hotel is of modern construction, built on an extensive scale, with accommodations for four hundred guests; beautifully located on Long Island Sound, fourteen miles east of New Haven, on the New London and Stonington Railroad; new Billiard Room, with three new tables, two new ten-pin alleys at a convenient distance from the house, and twelve new Bathing Houses. Fishing is not surpassed on the Sound. A new yacht of forty-five tons, and several small sail boats, will be constantly on hand, ready for parties.

Going from New York to Sachem's Head, take the 8 A. M. train and 3 P. M. train; *check and ticket* to Sachem's Head direct, changing cars at New Haven—time through 3½ hours. From New Haven to the Head at 7¼ A. M., 11 A. M., and 6 P. M.—time forty minutes. At the Sachem's Head depot will be found one of Cook's best four-horse Omnibuses, new and clean, to carry you direct to the House.

A new Barn, one hundred by fifty-two feet, has been built this Spring, which will accommodate fifty horses. Eight acres of land have been enclosed and filled with ornamental and fruit trees, walks, &c.

The House will be opened for the reception of company on the 20th day of June next, under the immediate superintendence of the owner.

N. B.—Mosquitoes are never seen at the Head.

May 23, 1860.

H. LEE SCRANTON.

G. & D. COOK & CO.

No. 35.

Eureka Jump Seat.

No. 35 B.

EUREKA JUMP SEAT.

ELAM HULL'S SONS'
IMPROVED
REFINED CANDLES,
WITH PATENT WICK,

Extensively and favorably known for nearly half a Century as superior to any other article of the kind in the Market.

They are neatly put up in 20-lb. paper-covered packages, and are warranted to stand any climate in the world, and to give full satisfaction.

All orders must be addressed to the Manufacturers direct, and will receive immediate attention.

ELAM HULL'S SONS,
10, 12 & 14 BROADWAY,
NEW HAVEN, CONNECTICUT.

G. & D. COOK & CO.

No. 36.

ANTIQUE NO TOP.

COLLEGIATE AND COMMERCIAL INSTITUTE,
WOOSTER SQUARE, NEW HAVEN, CONNECTICUT.

This Institution has been in successful operation for fifteen years. It is designed to meet the wants of those parents who wish to secure for their sons all the advantages for mental education that can be anywhere furnished, without losing that attention to health and that parental supervision and government which the young require.

THE MENTAL TRAINING includes a thorough English, Mathematical, and Scientific Education, in reference to a complete preparation for any business that does not require the instruction of the Law, Medical, or Theological Schools; a course of classical studies, minute, thorough, and as extended as may be desired; a course of Modern Languages under native teachers; a course of History, and a course of Mental and Political Science.

THE MORAL EDUCATION is secured by the personal influence of the Teachers, by graduated disciplinary measures designed to insure speedy improvement or an early exclusion from the School, and by the systematic study of the Bible, of Moral Science, and of the evidences of Natural and Revealed Religion.

THE PHYSICAL TRAINING consists of a prescribed course of exercises in a large and well-furnished gymnasium, under the direction of an accomplished gymnast; and of such an amount of military drilling, under full organization as an infantry corps, with competent officers and instructors, as will secure bodily vigor, habits of command and obedience, and a kind and degree of knowledge which may be essential to the full discharge of the duties of a citizen.

Lessons in Swimming are made a part of the physical instruction during the Summer session.

Ample facilities are furnished for bathing, rowing, and bowling. Wholesome, athletic games, are carefully encouraged, and opportunities are allowed for occasional pedestrian excursions.

The Farm connected with the Institute furnishes a pleasant resort for the pupils, and an opportunity to see the practical operations of husbandry, and to engage in them as far as may be desired.

WM. H. RUSSELL, Principal.　　　　　　　　　　　　　　　　**F. C. SELDEN, Vice-Principal.**

G. & D. COOK & CO.

No. 37.

ANTIQUE TOP.

MISS DUTTON'S
Boarding & Day School for Young Ladies,
GROVE HALL, NEW HAVEN, CONN.

J. W. ORR N.Y.

This School was commenced nearly forty years ago, by Miss PETERS and Mrs. BIRCH, and, after being under their care for twenty years, passed into the hands of the present Principal. It is therefore one of the oldest Boarding Schools in the country and has an established character.

It has, besides the Principal, a full corps of good teachers in all departments. A lady of superior culture, born and educated in France, resides in the family and instructs in the French language.

The department of Music is under the instruction of Prof. STŒCKEL, Teacher of Music in Yale College.

Ten years since the house was enlarged to more than twice its former size, so that it affords airy and pleasant rooms for the pupils, and large and commodious school rooms.

The school-year commences the middle of September, and continues until the 1st of July.

For Circulars giving the terms of tuition, &c., apply to the Principal, Miss MARY DUTTON, New Haven, Conn.

G. & D. COOK & CO.

No. 38.

DOCTOR'S PHAETON.

ALLYN HOUSE

Corner Asylum & Trumbull Sts., Hartford, Conn.

CHAS. DEVENS, Jr., Proprietor.

No. 39.

Park Phaeton.

BRUFF, BROTHER & SEAVER,

IMPORTERS AND JOBBERS OF

FOREIGN & AMERICAN HARDWARE,

CUTLERY AND GUNS,

ALSO, RIFLES AND DERRINGER PISTOLS,

B. B. & S. OVAL EYE COTTON HOES,

384 & 386 BROADWAY,

RICHARD P. BRUFF,
CHARLES BRUFF,
G. ARTHUR SEAVER.

NEW YORK.

JAMES I. DAY,
(Special Partner,)
Late of New Orleans.

Sole Agents for R. P. Bruff's Cast Steel Axes.

No. 41.

Victoria Buggy.

Patent Claims

UNITED STATES PATENT OFFICE,

Hon. Philip F. Thomas, Commissioner.

AMERICAN AND EUROPEAN

PATENT AGENCY OFFICES

OF

MESSRS. MUNN & CO.,

IN ASSOCIATION WITH HON. CHARLES MASON, LATE COMMISSIONER OF PATENTS,

OFFICE OF THE SCIENTIFIC AMERICAN,

No. 37 PARK ROW, NEW YORK.

Messrs. MUNN & CO. respectfully give notice that, in addition to their own experience of nearly fifteen years' standing as Solicitors of Patents, they have associated with them HON. JUDGE MASON, who was for several years Commissioner of Patents. This arrangement renders their organization thorough and complete, and is a sure guarantee that all business connected with the Examination of Inventions, Specifications, Drawings, Rejected Cases, Interferences, Extensions, Caveats, Opinions upon Questions of the Validity of Patents, and Infringements, will receive prompt and careful attention.

PAMPHLET OF ADVICE

How to Secure Letters Patent, furnished free.

All Communications considered confidential.

Immediately after the appointment of Mr. Holt to the office of Postmaster-General of the United States he addressed to us the subjoined very gratifying testimonial:

Messrs. MUNN & CO.: It affords me much pleasure to bear testimony to the able and efficient manner in which you discharged your duties as Solicitors of Patents while I had the honor of holding the office of Commissioner. Your business was very large, and you sustained (and, I doubt not, justly deserved) the reputation of energy, marked ability, and uncompromising fidelity in performing your professional engagements. Very respectfully,

Your obedient servant,   J. HOLT.

Messrs. MUNN & CO.—Gentlemen: It gives me much pleasure to say that, during the time of my holding the office of Commissioner of patents, a very large proportion of the business of inventors before the

Patent Office was transacted through your agency, and that I have ever found you faithful and devoted to the interests of your clients, as well as eminently qualified to perform the duties of Patent Attorneys with skill and accuracy. Very respectfully,

Your obedient servant,   WM. D. BISHOP.

It would require many columns to detail all the ways in which the inventor or patentee may be served at our offices. We cordially invite all who have anything to do with patent property or inventions to call at our extensive offices, 37 Park Row, New York, where any questions regarding the rights of patentees will be cheerfully answered. Communications and remittances by mail, and models by express (pre-paid), should be addressed to

MUNN & CO., No. 37 Park Row, New York.

INVENTORS, MACHINISTS, MILLWRIGHTS, AND MANUFACTURERS.

The SCIENTIFIC AMERICAN is a paper peculiarly adapted to all persons engaged in these pursuits, while to the Farmer, Housekeeper, and Man of Science, it will be found of equal interest and use.

The SCIENTIFIC AMERICAN has been published FOURTEEN YEARS, and has the largest circulation of any journal of its class in the world. It is indispensable to the Inventor and Patentee; each number containing a complete official list of the claims of all the patents issued each week at the United States Patent Office, besides elaborate notices of the most important inventions, many of which are accompanied with engravings executed in the highest degree of perfection.

To the Mechanic and Manufacturer the SCIENTIFIC AMERICAN is important, as every number treats of matters pertaining to their business, and as often as may be deemed necessary a column or two on the metal and lumber markets will be given; thus comprising, in a useful, practical, scientific paper, a Price Current which can be relied upon.

The SCIENTIFIC AMERICAN is published weekly in a form suitable for binding, each number containing sixteen pages of letter-press, with numerous illustrations, making a yearly volume of 832 pages of useful matter not contained in any other paper.

TERMS.—To mail subscribers: Two Dollars a Year or One Dollar for Six Months. One Dollar pays for one complete volume of 416 pages; two volumes comprise one year. The volumes commence on the first of JANUARY and JULY.

CLUB RATES.—Five Copies, for Six Months, $4. Ten Copies, for Six Months, $8. Ten Copies, for Twelve Months, $15. Fifteen Copies, for Twelve Months, $22. Twenty Copies, for Twelve Months, $28. Specimen copies will be sent gratis to any part of the country.

Southern, Western, and Canadian money or Post-office stamps taken at par for subscriptions. Canadian subscribers will please to remit twenty-six cents extra on each year's subscription to pre-pay postage.

MUNN & CO,

Publishers, No. 37 Park Row, New York.

G. & D. COOK & CO.

No. 42.

Plantation No Top.

CATARACT
WASHING MACHINE.

DESCRIPTION.

It consists of a metal cylinder, with cleets on the inner surface, and an interior cylinder of wood, with cleets. There is a space of from six to eight inches between the two cylinders. One crank turns both cylinders at the same time in opposite directions, rapidly creating a suds, forcing the water through the clothes, and effectually removing the dirt.

ADVANTAGES.

This Machine dispenses entirely with the washboard. THE *action of the water* CLEANS THE CLOTHES, consequently there is NO WEAR OF FABRIC. The *saving of clothing*, and the *saving of time and labor*, are equally remarkable. The Machine is simple in construction and management,—a child can use it. It is well made, of galvanized iron, and is very durable. It will wash the *finest* as well as the coarsest fabrics,—a single small piece, or a quantity of clothing. For Flannels (usually the most difficult things for the laundress to manage), its operation is astonishing, as it thoroughly cleans them, with no possibility of shrinkage.

Prices.—No. 1, $12; No. 2, $14; No. 3, $16.

Machines can be seen in operation at No. **494 Broadway**, east side, above Broome St. Ladies and gentlemen are invited to call and examine it, or, *what is better,*

☞ Send your Dirty Clothes and test it. ☜

SULLIVAN & HYATT, Proprietors,

IMPORTERS AND DEALERS IN

American & Foreign Hardware,

54 BEEKMAN STREET, NEW YORK.

No. 43.

PLANTATION TOP.

DAVID COOK'S
Fruit Basket

PAT^D. JULY 12, 1859.

MANUFACTURED BY G. L. COOK & CO.

NEW HAVEN, C^T.

We beg to call your attention to an article patented July 12th, 1859, and specifically designed for the sale and transportation of all kinds of Berries—at the same time point you to some of the prominent advantages which are conceded by all to whose notice it has been brought.

So unanimous are opinions in its favor that we think we are fully warranted in saying it is destined to supersede everything at present in use, and stand entirely without a competitor in the future. For several years past constant exertions have been made, and many devices resorted to, on the part of various parties who are largely interested in this trade, to do away with tight boxes, which, thus far, has been unsuccessful. But it is believed, and verified by actual experiment, that all the requisite qualities essential to the preservation of fruit, protection from bruising, &c. are concentrated in this invention. All concur upon the one point, that fruit, to retain its fresh, natural color, *must have " air."* And thousands of dollars are lost to the producers every season, simply from depreciation of fruits while in transit, or remaining a few hours too long, as they many times do, waiting sale in a depressed market.

Fruit packed in close boxes is in a most unnatural state indeed, the superficial moisture not being permitted to escape by evaporation. The air around it soon becomes damp and fetid, giving to the fruit a pale, unhealthy appearance, materially depreciating its market value, and, if not immediately cared for, accumulates the white mould, or undergoes a more serious change, *"rot,"* and becomes a total loss. In obviating this difficulty alone, (which is vital to all producers,) it is thought the article must commend itself directly to those who have given the subject a thought. Yet there are very many other considerations, comparatively of not less importance, aside from ventilation, such as facilitating the exhibition of choice fruits, neatness, beauty, symmetry, lightness, compactness, apparent excess of measure, &c., &c., all of which have a tendency to give fruit a choice appearance, enliven sales, and enhance prices. We are prepared to furnish, at short notice, pint and quart baskets, in quantities to suit purchasers, as follows:

Nett {
Pints, $30.00 per thousand.
Qts., $35.00 "   "
Open Crates, $1.50 each, (51 qt. capacity.)
Close Crates, $2.00 each, (54 qt. capacity.)
}

Ordinary Crates of 51 qts. capacity are a beautiful package,—extremely light, weighing less than 30 pounds, occupying a space of only 31¾ inches long, 15 inches wide, 15¾ high ; and a package of pints (64 baskets) occupies about the same space, and perhaps a trifle heavier. Baskets furnished with or without crates, as parties may desire.

Respectfully, Yours, **L. F. PINGREE,** *General Agent,*

To whom orders should be addressed, care of G. L. COOK & CO., 47 Church Street, New Haven, Conn.

ORDERS FOR CHOICE STRAWBERRY PLANTS OF THE BEST VARIETIES PROMPTLY FILLED.

G. & D. COOK & CO.

No. 44.

MEDIUM NO TOP.

KIMBALL'S IMPROVED CARRIAGE TOP PROP.

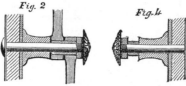

Fig. 1   *Fig. 3*

Fig. 2   *Fig. 4*

Fig. 1—Showing the prop as fitted to the top with DOUBLE JOINTS.

Fig. 3—Shows the prop as fitted to the top with ONE JOINT.

Figs. 2 & 4—Showing the prop as cut into in the centre, giving a view of the pipe which makes the shoulder for the nut.

PATENTED   DEC. 27, 1859.

THE SAFEST, NEATEST, CHEAPEST, AND BEST PROP EVER USED.

The advantages of this Prop over any other must be obvious to all who see it. But we will briefly state a few of them:

"It is the safest"—1st. Because we use a bolt and nut made of the very best Norway iron. 2d. Because, by using the pipe on the bolt, it makes a shoulder to screw the nut against, which allows of the joints working freely without loosening the nut. 3d. By putting the bolt through the Bow, the liability of the prop getting loose is entirely obviated.

"The neatest"—Because it admits of a small nut, and makes a perfect finish.

"The cheapest"—1st. Because the trimmer has got to make no calculations for his prop, but put on his Top as though there was to be no prop, thus enabling him to make a perfectly smooth job, then simply putting on the prop to suit the joint. 2d. Because much labor and at least sixteen screws are saved.

"The *Best*."—1st. Because it combines all that is useful in any other prop, without any of the objections. 2d. Because its combination is such that there is no probability of loosing the nut, which is a very great advantage over any other Top prop ever used. 3d. Because it will not allow the joints to rattle.

Price 33 cents per set, with a liberal discount to wholesale dealers. Capped Nuts and Rivets of all patterns, furnished to order, at the lowest prices. ☞ *All orders addressed to us will receive prompt attention.* For sale by all dealers in Carriage Furnishing Goods.

C. COWLES & CO.,
SOLE MANUFACTURERS AND GENERAL AGENTS,
27 & 29 ORANGE STREET, NEW HAVEN, CONN.

G. & D. COOK & CO.

No. 45.

MEDIUM TOP.

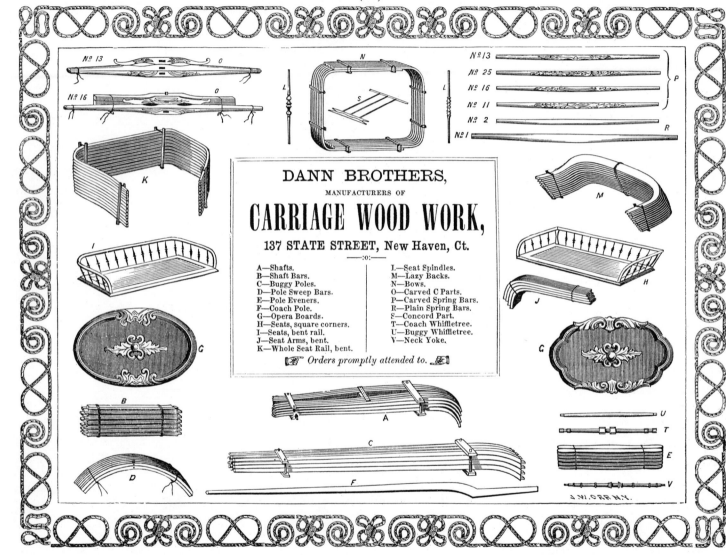

DANN BROTHERS,

MANUFACTURERS OF

CARRIAGE WOOD WORK,

137 STATE STREET, New Haven, Ct.

—:0:—

A—Shafts.
B—Shaft Bars.
C—Buggy Poles.
D—Pole Sweep Bars.
E—Pole Eveners.
F—Coach Pole.
G—Opera Boards.
H—Seats, square corners.
I—Seats, bent rail.
J—Seat Arms, bent.
K—Whole Seat Rail, bent.

L—Seat Spindles.
M—Lazy Backs.
N—Bows.
O—Carved C Parts.
P—Carved Spring Bars.
R—Plain Spring Bars.
S—Concord Part.
T—Coach Whiffletree.
U—Buggy Whiffletree.
V—Neck Yoke.

☞ *Orders promptly attended to.* ☜

G. & D. COOK & CO.

No. 46.

CUT UNDER NO TOP.

E. WHITNEY'S
IMPROVED FIRE ARMS
WHITNEYVILLE, 2 MILES NORTH OF NEW HAVEN, CT. U.S.

WHITNEY'S Revolvers are equal to any in market, and sold at less price. They are made of best materials and in a superior manner. Besides being better balanced, they are more accurate shooters than the old style of repeating pistols most in use; because the barrel is more firmly held to the cylinder, so that there is no yielding, and the centre pin, as should always be the case, is used only for the revolution of the cylinder. Whitney's new model pistols are warranted safe, efficient, and durable in all respects, if properly used. Calibre same as Colt's. Whitney's new model Mississippi and Minnie Rifles and Muskets offered on very reasonable terms. See the recommendation of Col. Jefferson Davis, late Sec. at War. Kit Carson says, Whitney's Rifles are the best to cross the Plains with. For further particulars and prices, send for circulars.

G. & D. COOK & CO.

No. 47.

FARMERS' BUGGY.

BRIDGEPORT NURSERY,

(Two Miles North of the City of Bridgeport,)

FAIRFIELD, CT.

LINDLEY & HINKS, Proprietors.

WE INVITE ATTENTION TO OUR EXTENSIVE ASSORTMENT OF

FRUIT, ORNAMENTAL, AND EVERGREEN TREES,

GRAPE VINES, SHRUBS, ROSES, HEDGE PLANTS, &c. &c.

Which will be found to comprise the best varieties, and of best quality.

Particular attention given to **DWARF** and **STANDARD PEAR TREES** (of which many are from Two to Four Years old, and have been Root-Pruned, consequently, can be transplanted with safety) and **GRAPES,** of which we have good, strong plants of all the hardy, desirable varieties—embracing DELAWARES of Two years old.

We design to have always on hand the most desirable articles for fitting up first-class Ornamental Grounds and Cemeteries.

TREES, &c. packed suitably for safe transportation to all parts of the Union.

We are also Agents for DR. C. W. GRANT, of "IONA," New York.

Refer to S. HARTWELL, Esq., President of Bridgeport Bank; DAVID COOK, Esq., New Haven.

No. 49.

CASH BUGGY.

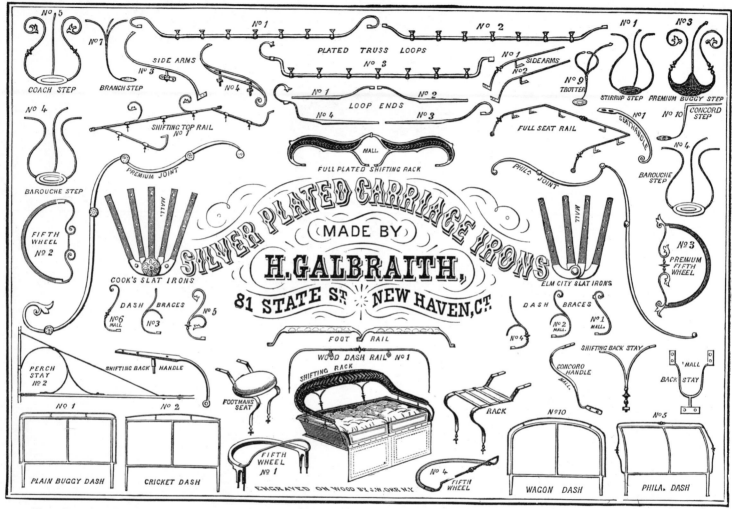

These Irons are all made from patterns now used by our first class Carriage Makers, and all except those marked "Mall." are forged from good iron by practical carriage workmen. Parties ordering will please order by *numbers*, and say whether they wish the Irons in *rough, common,* or *extra* plate, *spotted* or *full plate,* or *trimmed.*

☞ SEE ADVERTISEMENT ON PAGE 22.

G. & D. COOK & CO.

No. 50.

Student Buggy.

ST. NICHOLAS HOTEL.

[From N. Y. Pathfinder.]

When this vast and commodious establishment was opened to the public 6 years ago, it was confessedly the largest and most sumptuous hotel on this side of the Atlantic. The promise of convenience and solid household comfort, as well as of ease and luxury which its plan, arrangements and embellishments then afforded, has, it is believed, been fairly fulfilled. Time and experience have produced their legitimate results, in the shape of many improvements in the general management and appointments of the house; and the St. Nicholas of to-day is therefore not only equal, in all the elements of enjoyment, to the St. Nicholas of 1854, but has even stronger claims upon the traveling community, and as a family hotel of the highest and most modern class.

Covering nearly two acres of ground in the most eligible location on Broadway—nearly equidistant from the centres of the worlds of Business and Fashion—this establishment, with its magnificent front of 275 feet in length and five stories in hight, is one of the most conspicuous objects in the great metropolitan thoroughfare. It contains, in all, six hundred rooms; and on the second and third floors are one hundred complete suites of apartments for families, fitted up with every appliance of comfort and luxury which the most elegant private domicile could afford

One thousand persons can be commodiously lodged within the walls of the St. Nicholas, and in its three largest dining rooms six hundred guests can conveniently dine. The public rooms are superbly decorated and furnished; and in order to insure that *perfect quiet* which results from the noiseless movements of domestics, the corridors on every floor are carpeted from wall to wall with the softest tapestry fabrics.

The building, which is of fire-proof construction, is further secured against the possibility of danger from conflagration, by a special fire-police, with patent steam machinery capable of throwing one thousand gallons of water per minute, by which every floor can be flooded within six minutes from the first stroke of the alarm bell.

Steam is the great motive power in the domestic economy of the establishment. All the heavy work is performed by this agent; and in winter an even and healthful temperature is preserved throughout the interior, by its patent application to the purposes of heating and ventilation. To obviate the possibility of accident from this source, the boilers and furnaces are located in vaults, beyond the rear walls of the building.

A spacious private gas-house, capable of furnishing 200,000 cubic feet of gas per night, supplies the hotel with the material of light. This building, like the steam-generating department, is also detached from the main structure.

In order to afford the best attainable security against fire and robbery, every public portion of the hotel is kept under the quiet surveillance of a private police, whose duty it is to report at stated intervals to the principals or their representatives.

From the peculiar construction of the edifice, it is necessarily an eminently healthy establishment. The ventilation is perfect; circular galleries or wells running through all the stories from the second floor to the roof, where they terminate in ample skylights that can be opened and shut at pleasure, thus supplying pure air to every section of the building. This is a special feature of the hotel, of great importance to invalids, and will be appreciated by all who understand the value of thorough ventilation. Order, punctuality, and vigilant attention to the wants of guests are enforced in all the departments of the house, by means of a system of responsibilities running through the entire *personnel* of the establishment, and from which there is no escape. Under this regime, which is as strict and rigid as that applied in the administration of a city government — and perhaps *more so*, — the wants and wishes of innumerable guests are attended to with silent dispatch and without confusion.

The object of the proprietors of the St. Nicholas has been, and is, to combine in a hotel of the first magnitude all the elements of social and individual enjoyment which modern art has invented and modern taste has approved. Whatever has seemed likely to minister to the convenience, the comfort, and the amusement of their guests, they have endeavored, without reference to cost, to provide; and the patronage which the hotel has commanded during the past six years, is a gratifying proof that their efforts have been appreciated.

If doubts were ever entertained that a vast palatial hotel, like the St. Nicholas, would succeed in the Commercial Capital of the Union, they have long since been dissipated. It has been discovered that with a plan and organization commensurate with its capacity, an establishment capable of accommodating one thousand persons is not too large for a great and growing city; and as a proof that this idea obtains credit in Europe as well as in this country, it may be mentioned that agents have been sent over to the United States by the proprietors of fashionable hotels in London and Paris, to ascertain the plan, dimensions, &c., of the St. Nicholas.

Conscious that the present reputation of the establishment can only be maintained by making it as hitherto—attractive to the traveling world, the proprietors will spare no exertions to effect that object.

No. 51.

ELM CITY TOP.

MUNSON & SHELDON,

Attorneys and Counsellors at Law,

22 and 23 EXCHANGE PLACE,

NEW HAVEN, CONN.

COMMISSIONERS FOR THE SEVERAL STATES.

L. E. MUNSON,   J. SHELDON.

IN addition to the practice of the Law in all its branches, in the various Courts in the State of Connecticut, we have established a Collecting Agency, or department of foreign business. One of the members of the Firm will, from time to time, take such business tours through the United States and Canadas as may be required, for the collection of debts, payment of taxes, examination of land titles, and the transaction of business generally, where legal knowledge and skill, fidelity and thoroughness are required. Experience has shown us, that doubtful claims of long standing, may often be secured at small expense, by our personal attention and prompt measures, and that the expense of sending special agents, often without special qualifications, may be saved by business men availing themselves of the opportunities we offer.

Claims from abroad against parties in this State arranged, and avails promptly remitted.

WE SUBMIT THE FOLLOWING REFERENCES BY PERMISSION:

Hon. R. I. INGERSOLL, New Haven, Ct.,
Hon. E. K. FOSTER, " "
E. C. SCRANTON, Esq., President Elm City Bank, New Haven, Ct.,
H. B. SMITH, Esq., Cashier Merchants' Bank, New Haven, Ct.,
WELLS SOUTHWORTH, Esq., President City Fire Ins. Co., N. H., Ct.,
J. B. ROBERTSON, Esq., President State Fire Insurance Co., " "
G. & D. COOK & Co., New Haven, Ct.

Hon. R. S. BALDWIN, New Haven, Ct.,
Ex Gov. DUTTON, New Haven, Ct.,
Hon. JOHN WOODRUFF, M. C., Ct.,
A. H. McALLISTER, Esq., Cashier Quinnipiac Bank, New Haven, Ct.,
HENRY C. YOUNG, Cashier City Bank, New Haven, Ct.,
D. R. SATTERLY, Esq., President Home Insurance Co., New Haven, Ct.,
Hon. P. S. GALPIN, Mayor of New Haven, Ct.

FAIRBANKS.

STANDARD SCALES.

Adapted to every branch of Business where a correct and durable Scale is required.

Scales for Railroads, Scales for Coal Dealers and Miners, Scales for Hay and Cattle, Warehouse and Transportation Scales, Portable and Dormant Scales for Stores, Scales for Grain and Flour, Cotton and Sugar Scales,

Counter Scales of every variety, Bankers' and Jewelers' Balances, Farm and Plantation Scales, Weighmasters' Beams, Post Office Scales, &c., &c. &c.

All of which are Warranted in every particular. Call and examine, or send for an illustrated and descriptive circular.

FAIRBANKS & CO.,
189 BROADWAY, NEW YORK,
93 CAMP STREET,
NEW ORLEANS,
AND
16 SOUTH CHARLES STREET, BALTIMORE.

FAIRBANKS & BROWN,
118 Milk St., Boston.
FAIRBANKS & GREENLEAF
85 Lake St., Chicago.
FAIRBANKS & EWING,
Masonic Hall, Philad'a.

G. & D. COOK & CO.

No. 53.

NEW ORLEANS JUMP SEAT.

No. 53 B.

New Orleans Jump Seat.

THE BEST FIRE-PROOF SAFES IN THE WORLD !

Alum Patent FIRE & BURGLAR-PROOF, with Powder-Proof Locks.

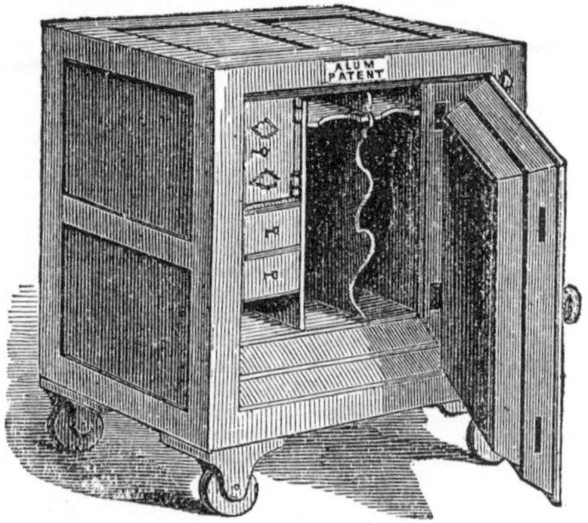

Plate and Jewelry Safes for Dwelling Houses.

SINGLE DOOR PLATE SAFES.

Plain, Lined with Velvet,

No.	Inside High.	Inside Wide.	Inside Deep.	Outside High.	Outside Wide.	Outside Deep.
1	18	15	17	24	20	23
1½	15	18	17	20	24	23
2	23	17	17	29	23	23
3	28	25	17	33	31	24

Ornamental and Imitation of Folding Doors, small Iron Vaults Inside, Case Lined with Velvet.

No.	Inside High.	Inside Wide.	Inside Deep.	Outside High.	Outside Wide.	Outside Deep.
1	26	23	16	34	30	24
2	41	23	17	48½	30	24

Plain, Lined with Velvet. Iron Vaults inside.

No.	Inside High.	Inside Wide.	Inside Deep.	Outside High.	Outside Wide.	Outside Deep.
1	26	24	17	32½	30½	24
2	31	24	17	38	31	24
3	37	29	17	44	36	24

Folding Door, Ornamented, and painted in imitation of Rosewood, Mahogany, etc., Marble Top and étagéres patterns.

No.	Inside High.	Inside Wide.	Inside Deep.	Outside High.	Outside Wide.	Outside Deep.
1	27	31½	17	35½	40½	24
2	48	29	20	56	36	27

HEIGHT OF CASTERS FROM 3 TO 9 INCHES.

Inside and Outside Dimensions (in inches), without Casters.

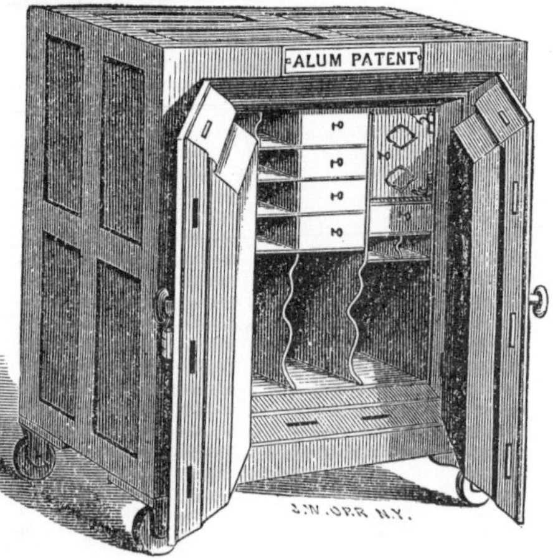

SINGLE DOORS.

No.	Inside High.	Inside Wide.	Inside Deep.	Outside High.	Outside Wide.	Outside Deep.
1	14	12	12	24	22	22
2	16	12	12	26	22	23
3	18	12	12	28	22	23
4	20	12	13	30	23½	24
Small Iron Vaults inside.						
5	16	16	13	26	26	23½
6	18	16	13	28	26	23½
7	18	18	13	28½	28½	24
8	20	18	13	30	28	24
9	21½	20	13	31½	30	24
10	24	20	13	35	31	24
11	24½	24½	13	3[illegible]½	35	23½
Small Iron Vaults inside, and patent Self-Lock ing Hasps over key hole on the outside.						
12	28½	24½	14	39½	35½	24½
12½	24½	28½	14	35½	39½	24½
13	32	24½	14	43½	35½	24½
14	37	24½	14	48	35½	24½
15	47	24½	15	58	35½	25½
16	52	24½	15	63	35½	25½

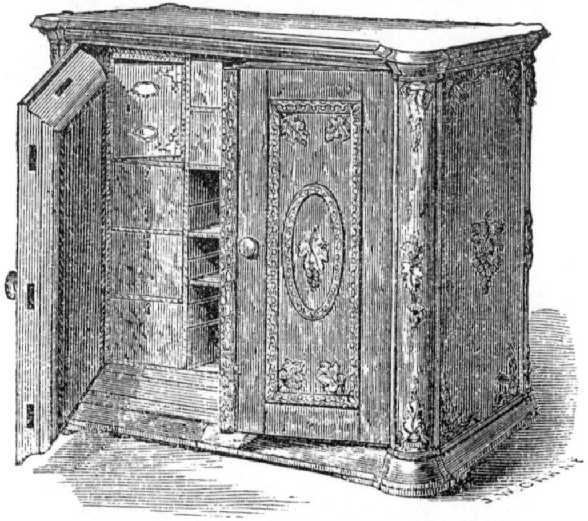

FOLDING DOORS.

No.	Inside High.	Inside Wide.	Inside Deep.	Outside High.	Outside Wide.	Outside Deep.
1	24½	34	15	36	45½	27
2	30	28	15	42	40	27
3	31½	33	15	44	45	27
4	35	33	15	47	45	27
5	46	24	15	58	35	25½
6	43	34	16	55	46	26
7	43	41	17	56	54	28
8	51	41	17	64	54	28
9	56	44	17	59	57	28
10	62	48	18	75	61	30
11	60½	56	18	72	68	30
12	66	60	20	78	72	32
13	72	64	20	84	76	32

The above are secured by Self-Locking Check Locks, throwing the bolts up and down at the side of the door. Iron vaults inside and patent Self-Locking Hasps on the outside of the door, requiring no key to lock the Safe.

Pamphlets containing full description of the **ALUM PATENT SAFE** together with Certificates, Price Lists, &c., sent to any address, post-paid, upon application. Orders from any part of the Union will be promptly filled. Safes delivered in New York free of charge. References to any party in New Haven or vicinity.

THOMSON & CO., 73 State Street, New Haven, Ct.

The largest Wholesale and Retail Store in the State. All Goods warranted as represented, or money refunded.

GOODS DELIVERED IN ANY PART OF THE CITY FREE OF CHARGE. ORDERS SOLICITED.

G.& D. COOK & CO.

No. 54.

JUMP SEAT BAROUCHE.

G. & D. COOK & CO.

No. 54 B.

JUMP SEAT BAROUCHE.

D. W. JOHNSON & CO.,

MANUFACTURERS OF EVERY STYLE OF

CHILDREN'S **CARRIAGES,**

W. H. DODD. SC.

HARTFORD, CONN.

SEND FOR CIRCULAR, GIVING FULL DESCRIPTIONS.

D. W. JOHNSON & CO.

MANUFACTURERS OF

TWO AND FOUR WHEEL

Children's Carriages,

AND PERAMBULATORS.

ALL GOODS DELIVERED AT NEW YORK.

Circulars, giving full description, sent to all who desire.

G. & D. COOK & CO.

No. 55.

QUINNIPIACK JUMP SEAT.

No. 55 B.

Quinnipiack Jump Seat.

THE PERFECTION OF ARTIFICIAL HEAT.

Fig. 1.—Boiler, Brickwork, and Regulating Attachments.

Fig. 2.—Sectional view of Boiler and Brickwork.

LOW PRESSURE, SELF REGULATING, STEAM HEATING APPARATUS,

GOLD'S PATENT, WITH L. M. HILL'S IMPROVEMENTS, MANUFACTURED AND ERECTED BY

HILLS & BENTON, No. 58 FULTON STREET, BROOKLYN, N. Y., & 88 & 90 STATE STREET, NEW HAVEN, CT.

(See Advertisements on Pages 122 and 124.)

G. & D. COOK & CO.

No. 57.

CRICKET.

HILLS & BENTON,

No. 58 FULTON ST. BROOKLYN, N. Y. & 88 & 90 STATE ST. NEW HAVEN, CT.

MANUFACTURE AND ERECT GOLD'S PATENT, LOW PRESSURE, SELF REGULATING,

STEAM HEATING APPARATUS,

IMPROVEMENTS.

WITH L. M. HILL'S

RADIATOR.

This admirable apparatus, as now perfected, is the only form of Steam Heating perfectly adapted to the warming of Private Residences, Stores, Churches, Hospitals, Hotels, Green-houses, &c. &c. The characteristic advantages are Economy and Durability in construction, Economy of Fuel, Entire Safety from fire and explosion (which can be said with truth of no other Steam or Hot-air furnace), self-regulation and ease of management, freedom from dust, gas, and noise. Even and quick distribution of heat, simplicity and durability, adaptation to all places, elegance of appointments where desired, freedom from unpleasant draughts of air, EFFICIENT and EASY VENTILATION, nicety of adjustment to any required temperature; it occupies but little space, reduces cost of insurance and fuel. This radiant heat is peculiarly adapted to delicate lungs, and in other cases where hot-air furnaces are open to great objections.

Call at No. 58 Fulton st. Brooklyn, N. Y. or 88 State st. New Haven, Ct. and examine for yourself.

A descriptive pamphlet, with figures, and numerous testimonials from well-known and eminent citizens, will be sent to any address, or given on application at either of the Offices, No. 58 Fulton st. Brooklyn, N. Y. and 88 State st. New Haven, Connecticut.

☞ *See Advertisements on Pages 120 and 124.*

G. & D. COOK & CO.

No. 58.

ROAD SULKY.

GOLD'S PATENT STEAM HEATING APPARATUS

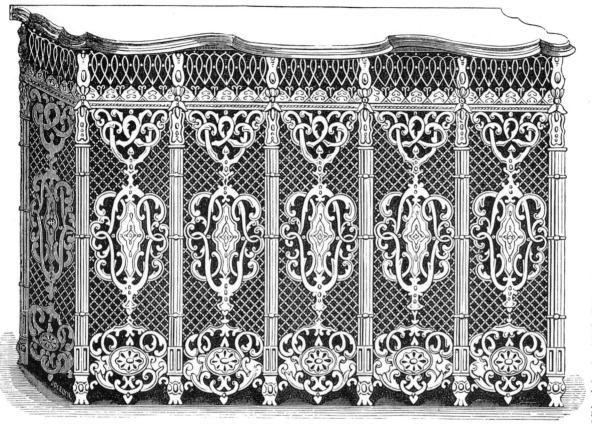

Fig. 3.—Straight-front Screen, for Parlors, Drawing-Rooms, &c.

HILLS & BENTON are permitted to r for the value of the invention to the lowing persons and places, where the paratus has been erected by them—as for the quality of their work, and th ability to discharge contracts:

E. W. Dunham, Esq., 65 W. Warren St., Brook
F. A. Platt, Esq., ... Clinton Avenue, "
R. T. Wild, Esq., ... 106 State St., "
Dr. Daniel Ayres, ...156 Montague St., "
Dr. C. L. Mitchell, ...77 Montague St., "
Dr. T. C. Durant, ...17 Strong Place, "
Nathan Southwick, Esq.,..122 Hicks St., "
J. W. Mason, Esq.,........120 Hicks St., "
H. Messenger, Esq., ...42 Willow St., "
Richard Field, ...109 Willow St., "
J. H. Cunningham, ..New York Avenue, "
R. R. Bennett, ...Fort Hamilton,
Thomas McElrath, ... Bay Ridge,
W. H. Dayton, ...North Orange,
George P. Smith, ... Cleveland, C
J. Punnell, ...
George A. Stanley, ...
Brown Brothers & Co., Bankers,.49 Wall St., N
Corn Exchange Bank,........13 William St.,
Phœnix Bank,................45 Wall St.,
Atwood & Co., Bankers, ...Broadway,
Bowery Savings Bank,..... ...130 Bowery,
Great Western Insurance Co.,..33 Pine St.,
Continental Insurance Co.,......16 Wall St.,
Arctic Insurance Co.,..........16 Wall St.,
New Amsterdam Insurance Co.,.14 Wall St.,
Columbian Marine Insurance Co.,14 Wall St.,
St. Vincent's Hospital,.............11th St.,
Ward School, No. 16,............9th Ward,
Cyrus Townsend, Esq.,...........Peekskill,
Rev. J. Trumbull Backus,..... Schenectady,
Prof. B. Silliman, Jr., Yale College, New Haven,
" E. Salisbury, " "
" F. Shepherd, " "
Wells Southwick, President City Fire
    Insurance Co.,.............. "
Charles Ives, Esq.,.............. "
James F. Babcock, Editor New Haven
    Palladium, ... "
James M. Townsend, Esq.,......... "
Seymour Bradley,................ "
C. H. Carter, Esq.,..............Waterbury,

The above are a few of the many references that might be added; for a more particular description, see a descriptive pamphlet, which will sent to any address, or given on application at either of the Offices, No. 58 Fulton St., Brooklyn, N. Y., or, 88 State St., New Haven, Conn.

MANUFACTURED AND ERECTED BY

HILLS & BENTON,

No. 58 Fulton Street, Brooklyn, N. Y.   88 & 90 State Street, New Haven, Con

☞ SEE ADVERTISEMENTS ON PAGES 120 AND 122.

No. 59.

WHITNEY WAGON.

AMERICAN WATCHES,

MADE BY THE

AMERICAN WATCH COMPANY,

AT WALTHAM, MASS.

TO THE PUBLIC.

Attention is invited to the following statement of facts in regard to these watches, and some considerations why they should be preferred to those of foreign manufacture:

Their sale has been constantly on the increase ever since the business was commenced—thus proving *that they have grown into popular favor through their intrinsic merits.* As an evidence of the extent to which they have received the endorsement of the public, we may state, that upwards of Thirty Thousand of them are now in daily use in the United States, giving perfect satisfaction to their owners.

This result has been effected in the teeth of the most determined and violent opposition from the greater part of those in the Watch Importing Trade in the large cities, who have systematically used all their influence with their customers, to discourage their dealing in an article which threatened, by its superiority, to displace the foreign watch to a very large extent. Many of the Jewelers and Watchmakers of the interior, a large proportion of them foreigners, seconded the efforts of the Watch Importers, being persuaded by their counsels, and misled by a contracted and imperfect view of their own interests; by the fear of loss on their stock of imported watches, and the apprehension that their profits might be diminished through competition in a well-known domestic article, with other groundless prejudices, arising from a superficial inquiry into the subject. Notwithstanding this, however, the watches have steadily gained in the estimation of the people, the retailers have been constrained to keep them to supply the demand, and by degrees, we are happy to add, their prejudices and alarms are being dissipated.

Our peculiar system of making the different parts of each watch the exact counterpart of every other watch of the same series, leads to a uniformity in quality which can never be attained by the foreign process. If one of our watches is good all are good ; whereas each foreign watch is only a probability by itself, depending upon the skill and fidelity of the particular workman who may happen to be employed upon it. In addition to these primary conditions of success, every watch issued by the Company is made of the most choice and enduring materials, carefully finished by the various processes to which they are subjected, and then put together, inspected and severely tested by the best workmen in the factory. Such has been the care with which these various duties have been performed, that out of the large number of watches sold, not more than a dozen or two have been returned to the Company for exchange, from any cause whatever.

Every watch is guaranteed by a guaranty that is good for something, and by parties that can be readily reached. Foreign watches, of the most inferior description, are often *fully guaranteed* by their makers, whom it is impossible to call to account under any circumstances.

American watches come to the consumer unburdened by the various expenses and profits incident to importation—the total of which, including custom-house duties, more than doubles the prime cost of the watch before it gets to the pocket of the ultimate owner. This consideration of itself should decide the question in our favor.

Every dollar diverted from the purchase of foreign watches is so much saved to the country ; so much encouragement to home industry, and so much added to the public wealth. We do not ask a preference on these grounds, if our watches are not *better* for the money than the foreign.

To conclude—we claim that our watches are the best and most durable time-keepers in the world, besides being the cheapest ; and we assert that a series of watches was never made that would show so little average variation from true time as those we have issued. In individual instances, their performance has been unsurpassed by anything recorded in the history of horology.

A descriptive pamphlet, containing full information and numerous certificates from well known individuals, may be had on application to the undersigned.

CAUTION.—As our watch is now extensively counterfeited by foreign manufacturers, we have to inform the public that no watch is of our production which is unaccompanied by a certificate of genuineness, bearing the number of the watch, and signed by our Treasurer, R. E. ROBBINS, or by our predecessors, Appleton, Tracy & Co.

As these watches are for sale by Jewelers generally throughout the Union, we do not solicit orders for single watches.

For the American Watch Company,

ROBBINS & APPLETON, WHOLESALE AGENTS, No. 182 BROADWAY, NEW YORK.

No. 60.

Boston Chaise.

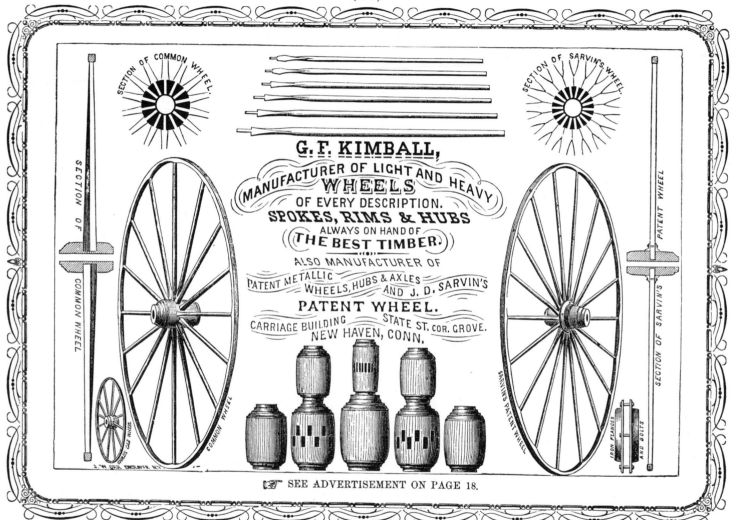

☞ SEE ADVERTISEMENT ON PAGE 18.

No. 61.

GAZELLE.

No. 62.

JAGGER.

No. 63.

Prince of Wales.

No. 64.

CHAMPION.

CHAMPAGNE AND CLARET WINES,

CORNWELL & CO.,

WHOLESALE DEALERS,

No. 103 WATER STREET,

NEW YORK,

Sole Agents for

SOUTHERN STAR CHAMPAGNE AND SPARKLING SCUPPERNONG.

ALL ORDERS PROMPTLY FILLED.

G.&D. COOK & CO.

No. 66.

DAYTON BRETT.

No. 67.

Child's Seat Drop Front.

CARRIAGE BOLTS   TIRE BOLTS   CARRIAGE BOLTS

COUNTERSUNK HEAD

WROUGHT IRON FELLOE PLATE

PLANTS
MANUFACTURING COMPANY,
PLANTSVILLE & NEW HAVEN, C.T.
ESTABLISHED 1842.

CARRIAGE BOLTS FROM BEST REFINED AND NORWAY IRON.

A. P. PLANT, PRES'T.   E. H. PLANT, SEC'Y.

PATENT NOISELESS

SHAFT COUPLING   SHAFT COUPLING   CLIP COUPLING

AXLE CLIP

SPRING BOLTS   PLOW BOLTS

CARRIAGE BOLTS   COACH SCREWS

ENGRAVED ON WOOD BY J. W. ORR N.Y.

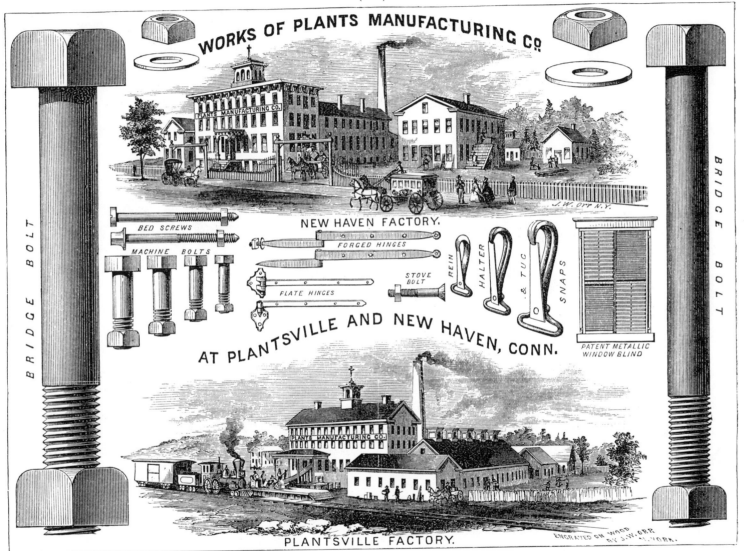

WORKS OF PLANTS MANUFACTURING CO.

NEW HAVEN FACTORY.

AT PLANTSVILLE AND NEW HAVEN, CONN.

PLANTSVILLE FACTORY.

BRIDGE BOLT

BRIDGE BOLT

BED SCREWS

MACHINE BOLTS

FORGED HINGES

PLATE HINGES

STOVE BOLT

REIN

HALTER

. & TUG

SNAPS

PATENT METALLIC WINDOW BLIND

J. W. Orr N. Y.

ENGRAVED ON WOOD BY J. W. ORR, N. YORK.

STIMSON, VALENTINE & Co., VARNISH MANUFACTURERS,
36 INDIA STREET, BOSTON.
FACTORY, RIVERSIDE, BRIGHTON.

A. G. STIMSON.　　　　　L VALENTINE.　　　　　H. C. VALENTINE.

No. 68.

CRESCENT CITY.

(136)

BARKER & BALDWIN,
MANUFACTURERS OF CARRIAGE BODIES

OF EVERY

51 BROADWAY,

DESCRIPTION,

New Haven, Conn.

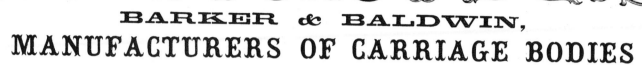

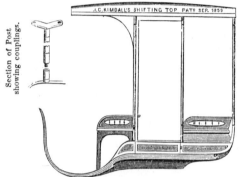

Section of Post showing couplings.

At our establishment, (the largest of the kind in the State,) may be found on hand, or made to order, a great variety of Bodies, such as Rockaways, from the lightest one-horse to the heaviest six-passenger, also Coach, Coupe, Brett, Barouche, Hearse, and Buggy Bodies of any desired style.

Having been engaged constantly for twelve years as practical Body-makers, becoming familiar with a class of work unsurpassed by any in the country, and having personal supervision of the work ourselves, and knowing that our reputation must depend upon the quality of our work, we say with perfect confidence, that we can serve customers with as good work and at as reasonable prices as any parties in the country.

We have, by recent arrangements with Messrs. G. & D. Cook & Co., secured the right to manufacture and sell Bodies with their "Patent Adjustable Seats," which have become so universally popular.

We have also secured the right to use J. C. Kimball's "Patent Shifting Top for Rockaways," by which the top can be readily removed for shipping, or to be used as an open carriage. The device is very neat and simple, and will be found a great advantage to shippers, as it will reduce the freight more than *one half.* (See cuts.)

We have recently perfected a plan of a rolling seat, by which a carriage can be changed from a one to a two-seat, and "vice versa," in less than half a minute. This plan possesses decided advantages over many of the adjustable seats now in use; and the Bodies are selling rapidly.

No. 1.—Ready for Use.

No. 2.—Ready for Shipment.

No. 1 of the above cuts represents one style of Body adapted to either "Cook's Jump Seat," or our Rolling Seat, or to Two Stationary Seats; it also has "Kimball's" Patent Shifting Top. No. 2 represents the same style with the top taken down, ready for shipment.

From the steady increase of our business for the last year we are led to infer that our work has given satisfaction; and it will be our constant aim, to make it for the advantage of parties in want of Bodies, Seats, &c., to give us their patronage. Selections of any style of Body represented in this "Chart," or elsewhere, sent to our address, with proper directions, will receive prompt attention, by

REFERENCES:

G. & D. Cook & Co., New Haven, Conn.
G. & H. King & Co., New Haven, Conn.
Durham Booth & Co., New Haven, Ct.

Hitchcock & Osborn, Richmond, Va.
Chas. T. Ward & Co., Macon, Geo.
G. C. Dickerman & Co., Natchez, Miss.

BARKER & BALDWIN.

JAMES P. BARKER.

CHARLES A. BALDWIN.

G. & D. COOK & CO.

No. 69.

Full Top Cabriolet.

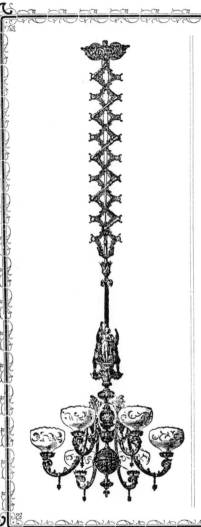

EXTENSION GAS FIXTURE

MONSON'S PATENT.

This well approved and unrivaled Fixture is manufactured and for sale by

STILLMAN MOORE,

CORNER OF STATE & COURT STS.,

NEW HAVEN, CONN.

☞ It is not too much to say that this is an article which may be recommended as quite the best, the most safe and durable Extension Gas Fixture in the world.

It is not a sliding tube. The extension is accomplished by the turning of tubes one within another, which are so protected against wear that even if the weight of the pendant were not counterbalanced, it could not come upon the tubing at all; and the ornamental levers which take the strain insure a uniform and beautiful movement.

The purchaser need have no fears of its leaking. It can also be attached to Chandeliers or pendants now in use. Testimonials like the following are voluntarily offered to any extent:

"After many months' trial of the above Extension Tube, we do fully concur in recommending the same as a well constructed and durable fixture, a most useful and excellent contrivance. We should be unwilling to exchange it for any other kind of Gas Fixture which we have ever seen."

IT IS ALSO FOR SALE BY

GEO. H. KITCHEN & CO.,

DEALERS IN GAS FIXTURES

AND IMPORTERS OF

Paris Fancy Goods, Parian, Bisque & Bronze Statuary, China Vases, &c.

No. 561 BROADWAY, NEW YORK.

N. B.—This Gas Fixture is recommended and adopted in the Government Buildings under sanction of Major A. H. BOWMAN, Engineer in charge, Construction Office, Washington.

No. 70.

SLIDE SEAT BUGGY.

MANNING, GLOVER & CO.

49 North Market St. and 46 Merchants' Row, Boston.

Manning, Glover & Co., Curled Hair Factory, Walpole, Mass.

MANUFACTURERS OF CURLED HAIR,

AND WHOLESALE DEALERS IN

Feathers, Mattresses, Moss, Husk, Palm Leaf, and Excelsior,

49 NORTH MARKET ST. & 46 MERCHANTS' ROW, BOSTON, MASS.

G. & D. COOK & CO.

No. 101.

GIPSY BRETT.

G. & D. COOK & CO., GENERAL FORWARDING AGENCY,

83 SOUTH STREET, NEW YORK,

HAVING ample facilities and appointments for the prompt transfer of all kinds of Freights in the City of New York, beg to announce that we shall spare no efforts to render this branch of our business reliable and efficient in all its details. The many flattering assurances received from Manufacturers and others, in various parts of the country, warrant us in believing that our endeavors heretofore have been appreciated, and in every respect consistent with their interests, as well as highly satisfactory to their Consignees.

OUR purpose will be ECONOMY and DISPATCH in the transfer, avoiding expense of STORAGE, giving especial attention to CLASSIFICATION and RATES. Forwarding by the cheapest and most expeditious routes (when left to our discretion), and by a proper diligence avoiding the delay and unnecessary expense incident to Freights passing through this and other cities, consigned only through Transportation Companies, and left to find their way as best they can to their destination.

WE have perfected arrangements with all the principal routes (rail and water) diverging from New York, by which we can make available to Shippers the lowest Pro Rata Tariff to all accessible points in the United States and Canadas, furnishing through bills of lading and prompt mail advices to Consignees, also Forwarding Agents, at points of necessary transhipment, with whom we are in constant communication throughout the South and West.

PARTICULAR attention given to Freights destined to foreign as well as domestic ports, by sail or ocean steamers; and custom-house clearances promptly attended to in all cases.

IN answer to the many inquiries, as regards the amount of Commission charged by us for the transfer of goods, we desire to state that for the better protection and dispatch of our own Freights, which amount to some five thousand carriages per annum, going to all parts of the country, we found it necessary, in 1859, to establish a Forwarding Agency in this City, entirely at our own expense; and the teams and appointments necessary to dispatch this business properly are found capable of performing considerably more at the same current expense. Hence we are induced to receive such an amount of Freights as will work our teams, &c., up to the fullest capacity, FREE OF COMMISSION, other than the legal rates for cartage as regulated by city ordinance and incident to all Freights transferred at this point, by whatever means, which, together with our facilities above alluded to, will, we trust, commend us to the favorable consideration of Manufacturers, Jobbers, and Shippers generally.

SHIPPERS, consigning to our care, can indicate their preference of line, should they desire, but it would be inadvisable to give POSITIVE INSTRUCTIONS, as contingencies are liable to transpire beyond their knowledge, at the time of Shipment, rendering it impracticable to carry them out, and we could not go contrary to definite orders.

INSURANCE effected when advised to that effect; also, **STENCIL PLATES**, of any required size, furnished on application.

☞ In all cases mark Packages care G. & D. C. & CO., N. Y.

G. & D. COOK & CO.

No. 102.

COUPE ROCKAWAY.

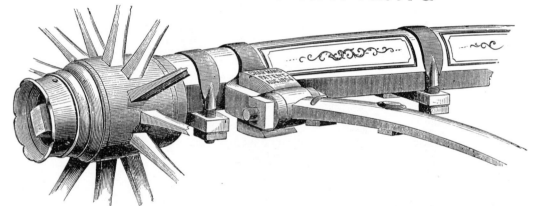

Chapman's
ELASTIC ANTI-RATTLING

THE BEST SHAFT COUPLING

IN THE WORLD.

CARRIAGE SHAFT FASTENER
PATENTED AUG. 8, 1854.

Used on all Light Carriages made by G. & D. Cook & Co.

All orders should be addressed to **W. S. CHAPMAN,** Cincinnati, O.

G. & D. COOK & CO.

No. 103.

A C SPRING COACH R

PORTABLE STEAM ENGINES.

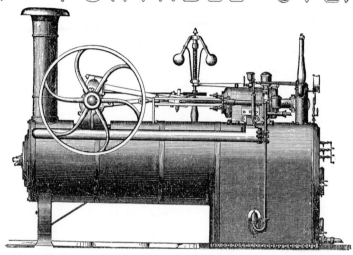

No.	Power.	Boiler.	Cylinder.		Speed.	Weight.	Price.
		Fire	Diam.	St'ke.	Rev.		
	H. P.	Surface. Sq. Ft.	In.	In.	per Min.	Pounds.	Cash.
1	2	22	3	9	175	2,200	$300 00
2	2	40	3	9	175	2,350	365 00
3	2½	47	3½	9	175	2,500	385 00
4	3	44	4	10	150	2,700	425 00
5	4	50	4½	10	150	2,900	450 00
6	5	60	5	10	150	3,200	475 00
7	6	90	5½	10	175	3,700	575 00
8	7	97	6	10	175	3,900	600 00
9	8	100	7	10	175	4,500	675 00
10	12	139	8	12	175	5,800	840 00
11	15	161	9	12	175	6,500	950 00
12	20	286	10	18	125	10,300	1,300 00
13	25	308	11	18	125	11,500	1,400 00
14	30	357	12	18	125	13,000	1,550 00
15	35	432	14	18	125	15,000	2,000 00
16	40	510	16	18	125	17,000	2,300 00

THESE Engines are very compact and complete, having a feed-water Heater, Force-Pump, Regulator, Belt-Pulley, turned on the face, Steam-Gauge; in short, every thing necessary to set them in operation, on the introduction of water and fuel, (either wood or coal,) to the boiler, and applying a belt. No smoke-pipe is furnished with them, as it is bulky, liable to injury if sent unboxed, and expensive to box up. Eight, ten or twelve inch stove-pipe, of heavy English sheet iron, is all that is required, and that is to be had anywhere, in any length the location demands.

The Boilers are of best American iron, strong, well made, and supplied with fusible safety-plug; and warranted to bear a cold-water test pressure of 200 lbs. per square inch, and a constant working pressure of 120 lbs. They embrace the principles of the best modern locomotives, are well made, without finish for show, and are capable of working much above the power inserted in table. Extra finish at extra prices. Our No. 10, Extra Finish, can be seen at the Varnish and Paint Store of STIMSON, VALENTINE & Co., No. 36 India Street, Boston.

The medium sizes, such as Nos. 5, 6, 8, 9, 10, 11 and 12 are always in progress, and can generally be finished to order in from three to six weeks.

☞ All Engines fired up and tried before they leave the shop, and warranted tight, safe, and in all respects ready for operation. Failing to give satisfaction, they will be taken back, and the money refunded.

A good strong running gear, arranged so as to be easily attached and detached at pleasure, will be supplied at from $125 to $225 extra—forming a useful wagon when separate.

ADDRESS,

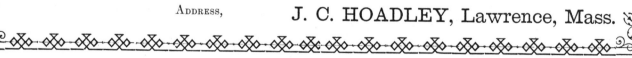

J. C. HOADLEY, Lawrence, Mass.

G. & D. COOK & CO.

No. 104.

HAMILTON COACH.

NEW HAVEN STEAMBOAT LINE,
1860.

FARE, $1.00. The First-Class Steamer No charge for Berths.

ELM CITY,
CAPTAIN LEWIS,

Will leave New York every day, (Sundays excepted,) at 3 o'clock P. M. Returning, leave New Haven daily, at 11 o'clock P. M.

NIGHT LINE.

The Steamer **TRAVELER**, Capt. BOWNS, will leave New York every night at 11 o'clock (Sundays excepted). Returning, leaves New Haven every morning at 10 o'clock. **Time, 4½ hours.**

RICHARD PECK, Agent,

Office over Fulton Bank, cor. Fulton and Pearl Sts.

G. & D. COOK & CO.

No. 105.

FAMILY COACH.

SMITH & BARLOWS,

BRIDGEPORT, CT.

MANUFACTURERS OF

BENT FELLOES,

Also every kind and description of

BENT MATERIALS FOR CARRIAGE AND SLEIGH WOOD WORK,

From the best Eastern ASH, OAK, and HICKORY.

Our facilities for obtaining choice timber and manufacturing are second to none in the world. As we keep constantly on hand a large stock, we are always prepared to fill all orders with promptness.

GOODS DELIVERED IN NEW YORK FREE OF CHARGE.

HORACE SMITH,   DANIEL S. BARLOW,   WM. H. BARLOW.

G. & D. COOK & CO.

No. 107.

Lawrence Brett.

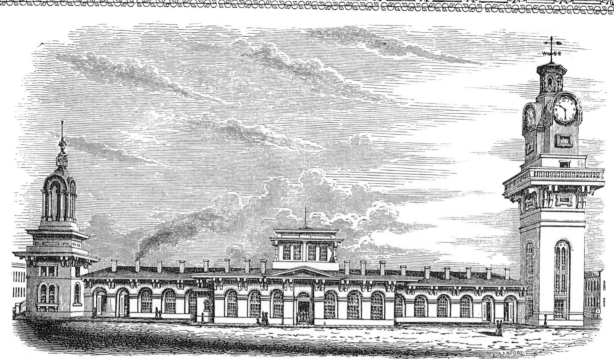

PASSENGER DEPOT OF SHORE LINE R. R., AT NEW HAVEN, CONN.

NEW YORK & NEW HAVEN RAILROAD,

Depot cor. 27th Street and 4th Avenue, New York.

Six Trains Daily each way.   Time, Three Hours.   FARE, $1.65.

No. 108.

LIGHT COUPE.

BRIDGEPORT
PATENT LEATHER
MANUFACTURING CO.
CANNON STREET,
WEST OF BROAD ST.
BRIDGEPORT, CONNECTICUT.

S. J. PATTERSON, Sec'y.

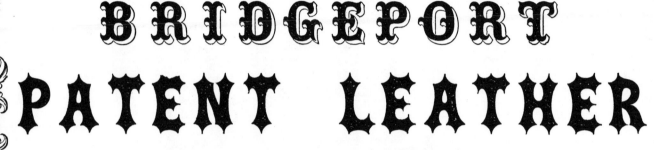

We have used large quantities of the Leather made by the Bridgeport Patent Leather Co., and consider it equal to any we have ever seen, and inferior to none in the market.

NEW HAVEN, June 20th, 1860.

G. & D. COOK & CO.

G. & D. COOK & CO.

No. 109.

CRANE NECK COACH.

SAVIN ROCK HOUSE,
WEST HAVEN, CONN.,
Situated on LONG ISLAND SOUND, 4 M. from New Haven.
Telegraph Office in the House.

E. A. UPSON,
PROPRIETOR.
Accommodation for 200 Guests; Sea Bathing,
Billiard Tables, Bowling Alleys, &c.

G.& D. COOK & CO.

No. 111.
LIVERY COACH.

GUANO.

SWAN ISLAND

ORGANIC, PHOSPHATIC, AND AMMONIATE

GUANO.

The attention of Planters and Farmers is called to this valuable Guano, which is claimed to be superior to any other imported fertilizer.

A trial will *prove* it to be the *cheapest and best concentrated manure in use.*

Imported only by

THE SWAN ISLAND GUANO COMPANY,

184 Water Street, New York.

G. & D. COOK & CO.

No. 112.

Shifting Front Rockaway.

THOMAS MANUFACTURING CO.

PLYMOUTH HOLLOW, CT.,

MANUFACTURERS OF

Sheet Brass, German Silver and Platers' Brass, Sawed Metal for Jewelers.

COPPER, BRASS, GERMAN SILVER & GILDING WIRE.

Special attention given to cutting and raising Blanks from any of the above metals for manufacturers. Facilities good as the best. A share of public patronage solicited.

No. 113.
PANEL QUARTER ROCKAWAY.

A. TERRY & CO.

MANUFACTURERS OF

Malleable Iron Castings,

TERRYVILLE, CONN.

ARE PREPARED TO EXECUTE ORDERS FOR EVERY DESCRIPTION OF

MALLEABLE IRON CASTINGS; CARRIAGE, CAR & HARNESS TRIMMINGS;

WRENCHES, CLEVISES, SCYTHE & CRADLE TRIMMINGS,

&c. &c. &c.

We have Patterns of nearly every approved style of Harness Trimmings; and will make with taste, at short notice, and at reasonable prices, Patterns for anything in our line, either from draft, description, or sample, for parties who may order our Castings.

We have had long and successful experience in the business. We have good facilities, and give our personal and undivided attention to every department of the work, and have no doubt that we can give satisfaction both in regard to quality and price.

ANDREW TERRY,　　　　　　O. D. HUNTER,　　　　　　R. D. H. ALLEN.

G. & D. COCK & CO.

No. 114.

Jump Seat Top Wagon.

GRAY & WOODS'
PATENT IMPROVED COMBINATION PLANER,

Patented Aug. 22, 1854, and Sept. 4, 1855, and Sept. 7, 1858, and Jan. 24, 1860. Reissued April 17, 1860.

This Machine is a combination of the WOODWORTH & DANIELS PLANER, and is calculated for all kinds of Shop Work. GRAY & WOODS are also manufacturers of all kinds of

WOOD-WORKING MACHINERY.

Send for Circular.   Address   **GRAY & WOODS, 69 Sudbury St., Boston, Mass.**

G. & D. COOK & CO.

No. 115.

Brewster Calash Coach.

GEO. E. WHITE,

55 CLIFF ST.,   **NEW YORK,**

DEALER IN   ALL VARIETIES OF

PURE NATIVE WINES

For the Table, for Invalids, or Sacramental purposes.

They are guaranteed to be perfectly pure, and Chemical Tests are invited.
N. B.—The best new hardy Grapevines for Vineyards or Gardens will be supplied to those who desire them.

GEO. E. WHITE,

55 CLIFF ST., **NEW YORK,**

General Commission Merchant,

Will make purchases of all kinds of Merchandise, or enter at the Custom House, and forward goods. Advances made on Consignments.

REFERENCES:

NEW YORK.—Wm. Bailey Lang, Esq., 54 *Cliff Street.*
BOSTON.—Messrs. Carruth & Sweetser, 25 *Broad Street.*
LONDON.—Messrs. Jacob Wrench & Sons, *London Bridge.*
LIVERPOOL.—John Carow, Esq., 11 *Lower Castle Street.*
PARIS.—MM. Vilmorin, Andrieux et Cie., 30 *Quai de la Mégisserie.*
NEW ORLEANS.—Messrs. Beebe & Co.
CHARLESTON, S. C.—Chas. D. Carr, Esq.

A SUBSTITUTE FOR PERUVIAN GUANO.

L. S. HOYT'S

AMMONIATED BONE

Superphosphate of Lime.

OFFICE, 194 WATER ST.,

ADJOINING UNITED STATES HOTEL,   **NEW YORK.**

THIS Superphosphate of Lime is a Chemical combination of the most active, durable, and valuable Fertilizers, mixed in the proportions that science and practical experience have proved to be the most beneficial to the Soil, and consists of Bone, Sulphuric and Phosphoric Acids, Ammonia, Soda, and Potash. It is of Uniform Quality.

I am permitted to refer to a great number of Planters who used HOYT'S SUPERPHOSPHATE OF LIME upon their crops of Cotton, Corn, &c., the past season, as well as Farmers and Gardeners, North and East, who have applied it for years to their various crops, with the most satisfactory results.

PRICE.—In New York, $45 per Ton of 2000 lbs. A discount made to buyers of five Tons or more. Packed in strong bags of 150 lbs. Barrels average 275 lbs. each.

CAUTION.—Observe that every bag and barrel of HOYT'S SUPERPHOSPHATE OF LIME is branded as above designated. None other is genuine.

☞ Send for a Pamphlet, containing Analysis, Directions, and latest Certificates; or further information may be obtained from my Agents.

☞ Pure Ground Bone, coarse and fine, packed in barrels, in good shipping order, for sale in any quantity.

G. E. WHITE will receive orders for Swan Island Guano, as advertised on page 158, and for Hoyt's Superphosphate of Lime, ABOVE DESCRIBED.

G. & D. COOK & CO.

No. 116.

Fall Scroll Brett.

GEORGE BROWN,

No. 274 CHAPEL STREET, NEW HAVEN, CONN.

Wholesale and Retail Dealer in

GOLD AND SILVER WATCHES,
Fine Jewelry, Clocks, Diamonds,
Sterling Silver Ware, Rich Silver-plated Ware,
GOLD AND SILVER SPECTACLES,
FANS, OPERA GLASSES,

GAS FIXTURES, and every variety of FANCY GOODS.
HAIR JEWELRY
Of every description made to order at short notice.

Society Badges
Constantly on hand, and made to order in the very best manner.
Designs furnished when required.

Strangers visiting New Haven are respectfully solicited to examine our assortment, which will be found very attractive, comprising all the *Novelties to be found in larger cities, at much lower prices.* Goods warranted in all cases as represented.

WATCH REPAIRING done in the most scientific manner by experienced workmen.

No. 119.

CARVED CHARRIOTTEE.

NEW AMERICAN CYCLOPÆDIA:

A DICTIONARY OF GENERAL KNOWLEDGE,

Edited by GEORGE RIPLEY AND CHAS. A. DANA.

To be completed in 15 Vols. royal octavo, large size, double columns. Vols. 1 to 10 are ready, and a successive vol. will be issued every 2 to 3 mos.

Price in Cloth, $3; Sheep, Library Style, $3.50; Half Morocco, $4; Half Russia, $4.50 each.

The design of this work is to furnish a popular dictionary of UNIVERSAL KNOWLEDGE. It will present accurate and copious information on Astronomy, Natural Philosophy, Mathematics, Mechanics, Engineering, the History and Description of Machines, Law, Political Economy, Music, etc., etc.

In the Natural Sciences the work will give a complete record of the progress of Chemistry, Geology, Botany, Mineralogy, etc., during the last 50 years.

The exposition of the principles of Physiology, Anatomy, and Hygiene will be prepared by eminent writers of the medical profession.

In History it will give a narrative of the principal events in the world's annals.

In Geography and Ethnology the brilliant results of the original investigation of the present century will be embodied.

In Biography it will not only record the lives of men eminent in the past, but will devote a large space to sketches of distinguished living persons, prepared by writers who, from locality, personal acquaintance, or special research, are most competent to do them complete and unbiased justice.

Agriculture in all its branches will have careful attention.

The Industrial Arts, and that Practical Science which bears on the necessities of every-day life, Such as Ventilation, the Heating of Houses, Food, etc., will be treated of with a thoroughness proportionate to their importance.

The work is intended to be one of *practical* utility, for every-day consultation. It will abstain from doctrinal and sectional discussions, but the History of Religious Sects will as far as possible be written by distinguished members of the different denominations respectively.

It is the aim of the editors to produce an original work, so far as its nature will permit, one which shall contain all information of general interest to be found in the best modern Cyclopædias, yet which shall have a character of its own, giving an original dress to those articles which have already been treated of in other works, and will also present a great mass of subjects which have never before been brought before the public in an accessible form.

Opinions of the Press.

From the Springfield Republican.

"While avoiding all the abstruseness of the large European compendiums, we believe it will amply satisfy the scholar, the mechanic, and the merchant, as it is intended to give the latest information on every subject treated of in its pages."

From the Charleston Courier.

"W. Gilmore Simms and R. K. Cralle are the chief contributors on the topics of Southern literature and literary history for the new Cyclopædia of General Knowledge, now in course of publication by the Appletons."

From the St. Louis Democrat.

"The value of this work to every man of intelligence and learning can hardly be estimated. Nearly every reading man can afford to purchase it; and it will surprise us if the new Cyclopædia does not find its way to the fireside of every intelligent family in the Union."

From the N. Y. Evangelist.

"The new Cyclopædia surpasses all others in the space given to our own country—its Natural features and resources—and to American History and Biography.

From the N. Y. Christian Inquirer.

"A work like the one in question can only soar above its predecessors by a freshness and clearness which *they* do not possess, but which it may, and, from what we know of the abilities of the editors and of the writers engaged in it, this work *will*, possess."

From the Boston Transcript.

"From a careful examination of the proof sheets so far prepared, and of the details, we have no hesitation in saying that never before, in the same space, or indeed in any form, has there been written in every department of useful knowledge such a complete compendium of what every one wishes to be informed upon."

From the Richmond Examiner.

"The work promises, from the contents of this first volume, to be the very latest, as well as the very best, of modern Encyclopædias."

From the National Intelligencer.

"The scientific articles are evidently the productions of learned and accomplished men. Many of the papers deserve especial commendation as presenting the latest developments in their various departments of research."

Specimen Volumes will be sent to any address, post free, on receipt of Three Dollars.

D. APPLETON & CO., PUBLISHERS, 443 & 445 Broadway, N. Y.

No. 120.

HOUSTON ROCKAWAY.

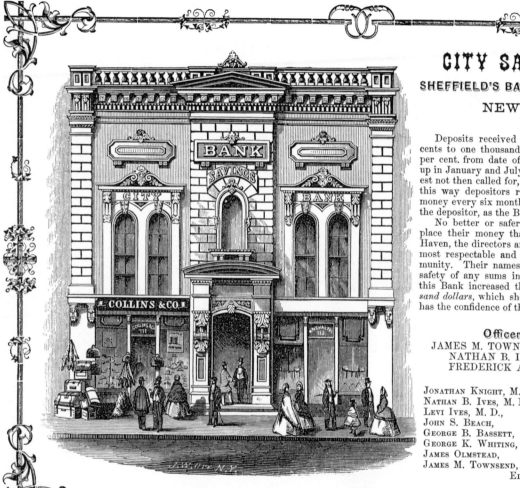

CITY SAVINGS BANK,

SHEFFIELD'S BANK BUILDING (UP STAIRS),

NEW HAVEN, CT.

Deposits received in this Bank every day, from five cents to one thousand dollars, and *interest* allowed at *six* per cent. from date of deposit. Interest account is made up in January and July in each year, and all sums of interest not then called for, will be added to the principal. In this way depositors receive compound interest on their money every six months, all of which is free from taxes to the depositor, as the Bank pays the taxes.

No better or safer place can be found for persons to place their money than the City Savings Bank of New Haven, the directors and officers of which are among the most respectable and prudent business men in the community. Their names are a sufficient guarantee for the safety of any sums intrusted to their care. Deposits in this Bank increased the past year over *two hundred thousand dollars*, which shows it is a popular institution and has the confidence of the community.

Officers and Directors.

JAMES M. TOWNSEND, *President and Treasurer.*
NATHAN B. IVES, M. D., *Vice-President.*
FREDERICK A. TOWNSEND, *Secretary.*

Directors.

JONATHAN KNIGHT, M. D.,	GEORGE COOK,
NATHAN B. IVES, M. D.,	DAVID COOK,
LEVI IVES, M. D.,	HUGH GALBRAITH,
JOHN S. BEACH,	SHERMAN W. KNEVALS.
GEORGE B. BASSETT,	SIDNEY M. STONE,
GEORGE K. WHITING,	AMBROSE TODD,
JAMES OLMSTEAD,	H. LEE SCRANTON,
JAMES M. TOWNSEND,	FREDERICK A. TOWNSEND,
ELIAS B. BISHOP.	

G. & D. COOK & CO.

No. 121.

LIGHT CALASH COACH.

FLORA TEMPLE, the "Queen of the Turf."

(OWNED BY WM. MAC DONALD, ESQ., BALTIMORE.)

FLORA TEMPLE is a light bay mare, 14 hands 1½ inches high, and weighs, in trotting condition, 835 pounds. Was foaled in 1846, in Sangerfield, Oneida Co., N. Y., out of Madam Temple, by One-Eyed Hunter; he by the well-known Kentucky Hunter. She made her first appearance in public on the Red House track, in 1850, beating the Waite Pony in a single mile dash; and in the same year, on the Union Course, L. I., under the name of Flora, won a race, mile heats in harness, beating Whitehall and three others. Flora has been entered ninety-five races—winning SEVENTY-FIVE, receiving forfeit in five, two drawn—and has beaten all the more celebrated horses known to the American Turf. In her renowned match with Princess, at Kalamazoo, Mich., in 1859, she made the wonderful time of 2:19¾, which is unequaled in the Turf records of the world, establishing, beyond question, her right to the title of "Queen of the Turf."

G. & D. COOK & CO.

No. 122.

CONTINENTAL ROCKAWAY.

LOSSING-BARRITT

GEORGE M. PATCHEN, the "Champion Trotting Stallion."

(OWNED BY DR. LONGSTREET, OF BORDENTOWN, N. J., AND MR. HALL, OF ROCHESTER, N. Y.)

PATCHEN is a deep blood bay stallion, full 16 hands high. Was foaled in 1849; got by the well-known stallion Cassius M. Clay. Dam, a celebrated Trustee mare,—her dam by American Eclipse. He was placed in the stud at Bordentown, in 1852, where he remained, with a brief exception, until 1858. During the latter year he was matched with several fast horses of the New Jersey Course, and defeated most of them with apparent ease. In 1859 Patchen trotted in several matches, on Long Island, with marked success, defeating many well-known horses, among which were the following:—Pilot, Brown Dick, Miller's Damsel, Lady Woodruff, and Lancet. In May, 1860, Patchen clearly demonstrated his superior trotting powers by defeating, in two races, the famous Ethan Allen; but the zenith of his glory was not reached until his memorable contest with Flora Temple, on the 12th of June, 1860, in which he defeated that world-renowned trotter, making his mile in 2:23, the fastest trotting time ever made by a stallion on the American Turf.

No. 123.

English Phaeton.

RATHBUN & CO.,

DEALERS IN

ANTHRACITE AND BITUMINOUS COAL,

No. 18 State St., New Haven, Conn.,

Have superior facilities for supplying manufacturers and all cargo purchasers with the following varieties of Coal, at the LOWEST RATES :

LEHIGH,	**SCHUYLKILL,**	Lackawanna,
Sugar Loaf,	Greenwood,	Scranton,
Room Run,	Pine Knot,	Pittsboro',
Spring Mountain,	Phœnix, } Red Ash,	and
Buck Mountain,	Palmer, }	Cumberland.

E. A. PACKER & CO.,

Miners and Shippers of the celebrated

SUGAR LOAF AND ROOM RUN LEHIGH COAL,

ALSO

SCHUYLKILL AND CUMBERLAND.

Offices: { 13 Trinity Building, New York,
{ 103 Walnut Street, Philadelphia.

RATHBUN & CO.

Will give their personal attention to all orders for

COAL

To be shipped by the various Railway Lines centering at

NEW HAVEN.

G. & D. COOK & CO.

No. 124.

FRENCH DOG CART.

SEELEY'S EMPIRE CITY

Camphene,
Alcohol,
Coal Oil,
Burning Fluid.

Camphene and Alcohol Distillery.

AARON SEELEY,

32 & 34 BURLING SLIP, NEW YORK CITY.

Tar,
Pitch,
Rosin,
Spirits Turpentine.

G. & D. COOK & CO.

No. 125.

Six Seat Germantown.

NOW READY:

HARTHILL'S ILLUSTRATED

POPULAR GUIDE BOOKS FOR 1860.

Each Complete in itself and sold separately at Twenty-Five Cents. Profusely Illustrated.

I.—THE HUDSON, CATSKILL MOUNTAINS, SARATOGA,

LAKE GEORGE, LAKE CHAMPLAIN, and CITY OF NEW YORK. Described and Illustrated with Fifty of the choicest scenes and places of interest connected therewith. Price 25 cents.

II.—NIAGARA FALLS AND SCENERY,

Together with Trenton, Genesee, and Montmorenci Falls, City of Quebec and Battle-ground, illustrated in a series of Thirty Engravings of the Scenery of those world-renowned districts, with copious Letter-press Descriptions of each place noticed. Price 25 cents.

III.—THE MISSISSIPPI, FROM ST. PAUL TO NEW ORLEANS,

With Descriptions of almost every City, Town, and Village throughout the entire length of the route. With 30 River Charts and 40 Engravings of the principal Cities connected with its Trade and Commerce. Price 25 cents.

IV.—THE ST. LAWRENCE, IN ONE GRAND PANORAMA,

From Niagara to Quebec—engraved from the Charts of the Canadian government, showing the Rivers, Lakes, Rapids, Falls, Cities, and Towns throughout the route of 600 miles—with Letter-press Descriptions and Engravings of scenes on the St. Lawrence, the Thousand Islands, and all the Cities in Canada. Price 25 cents.

V.—THE WHITE MOUNTAINS,

TOGETHER WITH THE CITY OF BOSTON AND VICINITY. The Letter-press Description of this Work was supplied by an eminent literary gentleman, who traveled through the entire district last July, for the special purpose of compiling it. The Publishers, therefore, offer it with confidence as the most recent, and decidedly the most useful, hand-book which has ever appeared connected with the White Mountains. Profusely Illustrated. Price 25 cents.

The above Works are all uniform in appearance, size of page, &c., and have been got up in the best style in every respect. The Engravings are from Photographs and Pencil-drawings, executed by some of the best engravers in the United States, and are faithful representations of each place and object. They are offered as the best illustrated, best printed, most reliable, and the latest Guide-Books to the respective districts. Any one purchasing the Series of Five, can have them bound into one of the handsomest volumes portraying the physical features of the country ever published.

To be had of all Booksellers and Newsmen throughout the United States and Canada, and on the Cars, Steamers, Book-stalls, &c., everywhere. Copies mailed free to any address on receipt of the price (25 cents for each) by A. HARTHILL & CO., Publishers, No. 20 North William Street, New York. The trade supplied by any Wholesale Bookseller or News Agent.

ALEX. HARTHILL & CO., Steam Printers,

20 North William Street, New York.

No. 126.

YORKTOWN ROCKAWAY.

ORNAMENTAL IRON WORKS OF PHILIP TABB,

522 BROADWAY, NEW YORK,

Opposite St. Nicholas Hotel.

ORNAMENTAL IRON WORK,

IRON RAILING, IRON FURNITURE,

IRON BUILDINGS,

Made to order and shipped at short notice. Constantly on hand, at No. 522 Broadway,

IRON BEDSTEADS, HATSTANDS,

CHAIRS, SETTEES, WASHSTANDS,

VASES, FOUNTAINS, SUMMER HOUSES,

RUSTIC SEATS,

FENCES AND GATES,

For Country and City Places.

ALL KINDS OF PLUMBERS' WORK.

SINKS
Portable
GAS WORKS,
made to order.
CONTRACTS
taken
for building
GAS
AND
WATER
WORKS
FOR
CITIES, TOWNS
AND
FACTORIES.

WASHBOWLS,
etc., etc.
Every description of
Machinery
CASTINGS
made to order.
IRON RAILING
of every description for
CEMETERIES
PARKS,
PUBLIC & PRIVATE
HOUSES,
VERANDAHS,
Etc., Etc.

G. & D. COOK & CO.

No. 128.

LOOP CALASH.

L. DECKER,
BILLIARD TABLE MAKER,
90 ANN STREET, NEW YORK.

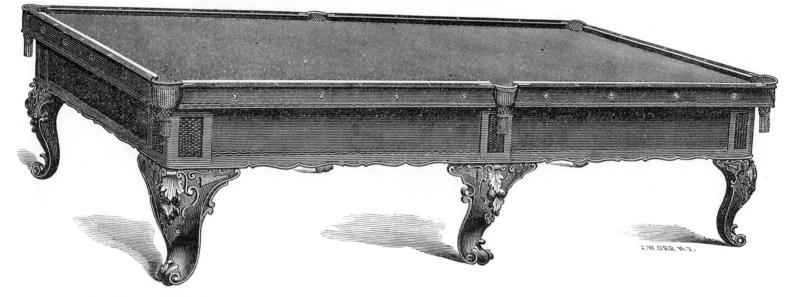

Six different sized Tables for private use; prices varying from $150 to $400, all Slate Beds, and finished in the best manner, with L. DECKER'S IMPROVED MECHANICAL CUSHIONS,

Patented November 9th, 1858,

the latest and best improvement ever made in Cushions, which will be made satisfactory by numerous references.

A full assortment of TABLES and TRIMMINGS constantly on hand.   Repairing done, &c.   Send for Circular.

G. & D. COOK & CO.

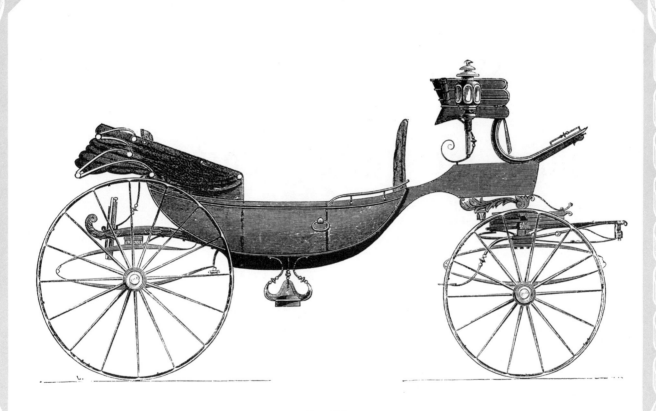

No. 129.

FULL SIZE CALASH.

TO PLANTERS.

SMITH BEERS'

PATENT

Machine for Pulling Cotton Stalks.

This INVENTION was Patented January 17, 1860, and is the best and only machine in the world for pulling Cotton Stalks, and is entirely new and novel in its operation. It is worked by two or more horses, and is capable of pulling and clearing twenty acres a day, and is so adjusted that by slipping in knives, fixed for the purpose, it will cut them in short pieces, or, without the knives, the stalks are left full length in rows, ready for burning.

ONLY ONE MAN IS REQUIRED TO WORK THE MACHINE!

It is very simple in its operation, and is not liable to get out of repair. The numerous testimonials received from the press, and from scientific business men who have seen the model and the operation of the machine, sufficiently demonstrate its utility.

The Patentee feels assured that there is *more real value and more money in this invention* than in any invention which has come before the public since that of "Whitney's Cotton Gin."

Town, County, and State Rights for sale.

By addressing the Patentee, full particulars will be given, with prices, &c. Address

SMITH BEERS, Naugatuck, Conn.

G. & D. COOK & CO.

No. 130.

CITY COUPE.

CHARLES PARKER,

MERIDEN, CONN.,

Sample Room, No. 15 Gold St., New York,

W.H. GREEN DEL & SC. MERIDEN. CT.

Manufactures all of the ordinary kinds of COFFEE MILLS; also, J. & E. PARKER'S PATENT UNION COFFEE MILLS and CORN MILLS; all kinds of PARALLEL VICES; a first-class SEWING-MACHINE of superior quality, making the double lock stitch; Parker's PATENT HINGES AND FASTENINGS for Blinds—universally liked; all kinds of BRITANNIA AND PLATED WARE; BRITANNIA SPOONS; IRON TABLE, TEA, and BASTING SPOONS; PLATED SPECTACLES and SPECTACLE CASES; PATENT TOBACCO-BOXES; and a very general assortment of DOMESTIC HARDWARE.

Call at No. 15 GOLD STREET.

No. 131.

FOUR SEAT GERMANTOWN.

VARNISH.

Upon page 134 may be found a representation of the extensive Varnish Factory and Business Warerooms of MESSRS. STIMSON, VALENTINE & CO., Boston, which are the largest in New England. But few years have passed since nearly all the Varnish used by New England Coachmakers and Painters was procured in New York, or imported from London, notwithstanding the fact that most of the gums used in its manufacture in this country were imported into New England. The above-named firm have demonstrated that Boston can compete with the best of them, and have produced Varnish the superior of which cannot be found this side of London, and is barely excelled by that. This Varnish has approved itself to artizans throughout the land, who have certified to its superior merit; and an immense demand has necessarily followed, which is constantly increasing. The Manufactory at Riverside is in constant operation to meet the great demand for Varnish,—from ten to twenty varieties comprising the list,—and from two hundred to four hundred gallons being produced daily.

The result of this busy manufacture is seen at Stimson, Valentine & Co.'s Great Warehouse, No. 36 India Street. Here the Stock is stored to ripen in cans, for which an entire loft is devoted. These cans, holding two hundred and seventy-five gallons each, are in number eighty-two,—besides which, ten tanks, holding one thousand gallons each, occupy places in this loft, showing an aggregate Stock of more than thirty-two thousand gallons.

The most perfect system being observed in storing it,—the date of manufacture of every gallon being registered and its location defined by numbers,—the purchaser may rely on receiving the precise article he samples.

Though Varnish is the great feature of the business of Stimson, Valentine & Co., their establishment in India Street is likewise a great Painters' Depot, where everything needed in that line is procurable—the lead and zinc, which are ground on the premises, the oil and spirits required to mix, the brushes with which to apply it, the glass needed for glazing, &c. Added to all this, they do a very large business in the refining and sale of Beeswax. From this store proceed those myriad hemispheres of clear, yellow wax, so much prized by shoemakers, sailmakers, &c., and that have also found their way into domestic use by their excellence of quality and reasonableness of price. The building wherein this vast business is performed presents a busy scene,—from cellar to attic men being engaged from morning till night in the several departments. Passing through the Cellar, the Store, the Retail Loft, the Varnish Loft, the Paint Mill and Engine Lofts, the Beeswax Loft, to the very top, we see a constant exhibition of activity and enterprise. A beautiful Hoadley Engine (see page 146)—the same that received the gold medal at the exhibition of the American Institute in New York—supplies the steam for rendering the wax, grinding the paints, warming the atmosphere to a fitting temperature for the Varnishes, and for operating an elevator that is constantly in motion, carrying goods up and down between the cellar and attic. Our brief space does not admit of an adequate description, and we can merely advise the reader to visit the scene and see it for himself.

G. & D. COOK & CO.

No. 132.

BROUGHAM ROCKAWAY.

DUNBAR & BARNES,

MANUFACTURERS OF

Cast Steel Skirt Springs, Coiled Springs, &c.,

Made from BEST CAST STEEL Plate (Watch-Spring Temper),

SKELETON SKIRTS, AND SKIRT MATERIALS OF ALL KINDS.

Manufactory, BRISTOL, Conn.   **Warehouse, 16 MURRAY STREET, New York.**

EDWARD L. DUNBAR.   WALLACE BARNES.

G. & D. COOK & CO.

No. 133.

SIX SEAT BAROUCHE.

ASA JOHNSON & CO., Patent Metallic House & Metal Roofing, Cornices, Gutters, Mouldings, &c.

FOR BUILDINGS, &c., MADE OF GALVANIZED IRON OR OTHER METAL.

The above materials are manufactured by the well-known firm of **MARSHALL LEFFERTS & BRO.**, 92 Beekman St., **N. Y.**

TO THE PUBLIC.—The attention is especially called to the new principle covered by the Patent for laying on the Roof, whereby the objection to the Metal Roofing, than any ction and expansion produced by heat and cold, is entirely overcome by this new mode of putting on and fastening, making a cheap and more durable Roof of contraother now used, and Water and Fire-proof; also, a safe protection against Lightning, saving all expense of Lightning Rods. Also, they are prepared to furnish Cornices, Gutters, Mouldings, &c., for buildings. All orders addressed to **ASA JOHNSON & CO., N. Y.**, will be promptly attended to.

G. & D. COOK & CO.

No. 134.

LOUISIANA ROCKAWAY.

WM. HALL & SON,

543 BROADWAY, between SPRING & PRINCE STS.,

PUBLISHERS OF MUSIC AND DEALERS IN ALL KINDS OF

Musical Instruments, and Musical Merchandise.

WM. HALL & SON'S New and Complete Catalogue sent by Mail, on receipt of 7 cents in Stamps. Music sent by Mail to any part of the United States, on receipt of the marked price.

DRIGGS' PATENT PIANO-FORTES,

OR

THE VIOLIN PIANO;

Recommended as the best Piano existing, by

WM. VINCENT WALLACE,   L. M. GOTTSCHALK,   WM. MASON,   WM. A. KING,
WM. H. FRY,   MAX MARETZEK,   S. THALBERG,   MAURICE STRAKOSCH,
HENRY SQUIRES, &c., &c., &c.

Letter from S. Thalberg.—"The tone is grand and noble. It has great capacity for sustaining the sound, or singing, and its volume of tone or power I have never heard excelled in depth, purity, and sympathetic sweetness."

Letter from L. M. Gottschalk, M. Strakosch, Wm. Mason, Max Maretzek, T. Eisfeldt, and others.—"The tone equals the best Grand Pianos, and exceeds them in pure musical intonation and actual tone power, thus approximating closer to what we consider perfection in the instrument than has yet been achieved by any other system of manufacture."

Letter from Wm. H. Fry.—"Your invention, in my opinion, is destined to work radical changes in the manufacture of Pianos, throughout the world. In a word, it is the best Piano existing."

Letter from Henry Squires.—"It gives a support to the singer I have never experienced, except from a well drilled Orchestra," &c., &c.

ALEXANDRE ORGANS.

The most perfect Reed Instrument in the world; adapted for Churches, Lecture Rooms, Schools, Lodge Rooms and Drawing Rooms.

Sole Medal of Honor at the Universal Exhibition of 1855.

This magnificent instrument, [patented in the United States, May 3, 1859,] which the brilliant performances of THALBERG, VILANOVA, and Mlle. WELLIS, have rendered as popular in America as in Europe, has been adopted by the greatest artists and composers of both continents—GOTTSCHALK, LISZT, ROSSINI, MEYER-BEER, &c., &c. The Alexandre Organ is celebrated for the solidity and precision of its mechanism, as well as for the fullness and power of its tones, and the remarkable quality of keeping perfectly in tune in all climates. Prices, $100, $160, $185, $235, $260, $300, $340, $400. They have from 5 to 16 Registers, and are equal in variety, power, and for all practical uses, to Church Organs costing three or four times the price of the Alexandre Organs.

HALL'S GUITARS—The best toned, most durable and reliable Guitars manufactured. They are warranted to stand the climate. The best Guitar strings. We will send a complete set of the best Guitar strings by mail, to any address, on receipt of 75 cents, in money or stamps.

WM. HALL & SON'S Flutes, Clarionets, Flageolets, Fifes, &c., &c., all finished in oil, and warranted. Fine Flutes, from $6 to $100. Diatonic Flutes, $45 to $125. Boehm Flutes, $85 to $150. *Every article in the Music Line.*

WM. HALL.   JAMES F. HALL.

G. & D. COOK & CO.

No. 135.

New Haven Barouche.

WALTER A. WOOD'S
IMPROVED MOWING MACHINE.

1st Premium Silver Medal, awarded by the United States Agricultural Society, at Chicago, September, 1859.

Price $80 for Two Horse Mower.
" 70 " One do. do.

DELIVERED ON THE CARS AT HOOSICK FALLS.

At the National Trial in France, on the Imperial Farm near Paris, June 19th and 20th, 1860, the *1st Premium*, 1000 *francs, Gold Medal, and Grand Gold Medal of Honor*, were awarded to

WALTER A. WOOD'S
AMERICAN MOWER.

WOOD'S MOWER.

P. CARD TROY.

F. RALLISON A & H

MANUFACTURED AT HOOSICK FALLS, N. Y.
(Patented February 22d, 1859.)

G. & D. COOK & CO.

No. 136.

SHIFTING QUARTER ROCKAWAY.

"The New Haven Patent Shirt."

Letters Patent Issued Dec. 21st, 1858; "Improved" July 4th, 1860.

JOHN PECKHAM,

CORNER OF COURT & STATE STS.   NEW HAVEN, CT.

PATENTEE AND MANUFACTURER OF THIS TRULY

NATIONAL SHIRT—THE SHIRT OF THE TIMES!

Would call particular attention to its many excellent qualities which make it so superior to all others and which have already, in so short a space of time, given it such a wide celebrity. It is made without useless seams and is therefore less likely to rip; is *not seamed or hollowed out* at the very point where *smoothness, room and strength* are so much needed—*on the shoulder ;* and is in every way the most stylish and well-balanced Shirt ever before offered to a discriminating public.

We are prepared to supply it in all styles and qualities, and would particularly like orders for samples from parties who wish to adopt some *one reliable style of Shirt for their whole trade.*

We will send sample half-dozens to those who order at same rates as per hundred dozen. Address

JOHN PECKHAM, New Haven, Ct.

No. 137.

ALABAMA SIX SEAT.

GEO. L. COOK,

No. 47 Church Street, New Haven, Conn.,

CIGARS,
Of the finest brands of my own Importation.

PATENT MEDICINES
OF THE DAY.
Agent for all the approved

ALCOHOL,
Camphene, Spirits Turpentine, Burning Fluid,
Kerosene Oil, Coal Oil, Potash, Borax,

DYE WOOD, DYE STUFF,
CONGRESS WATER, &c.

DEALER IN

DRUGS, MEDICINES, PERFUMERY,

FANCY GOODS, &C., &C.

No. 138.

Carved Turn Over Seat.

W. K. LEWIS & BROTHERS,

Manufacturers and Wholesale Dealers in every description of

PICKLES,	PRESERVES,	SYRUPS,	MUSTARD,
KETCHUPS,	JELLIES,	EXTRACTS,	HERBS,
FISH SAUCES,	PIE FRUIT,	CHOCOLATE,	PEPPER SAUCE,
MEAT SAUCES,	BRANDY FRUITS,	YEAST POWDER,	GROUND SPICES.

And Importers of

SARDINES,	SALAD OIL,	FRENCH OLIVES,	CAPERS,
ANCHOVIES,	GELATINE,	SPANISH OLIVES,	FRENCH MUSTARD.

Also extensive Packers of all varieties of

HERMETICALLY SEALED PROVISIONS,

such as

BEEF,	VEAL,	MUTTON,	VEGETABLES,
SOUPS,	POULTRY,	GAME,	FISH,
LOBSTERS,	OYSTERS,	CLAMS,	&c. &c. &c.

No. 93 Broad Street, Boston, Mass.

W. K. L. & Bro.'s are prepared to furnish a very superior article of Condensed Milk, combined with sugar, and manufactured under Borden's Patent, which is adapted for use on board ships, and for travellers generally.

No. 139.

LIGHT OPEN FIVE SEAT.

BAKER & GODWIN,

PRINTERS,

PRINTING-HOUSE SQUARE, NEW YORK.

☞ This is one of the Largest General Printing Establishments in the Union, and possesses unsurpassed facilities in Extensive Premises, Steam Presses, and Superior Machinery, every variety of Type, Engravings, &c., for the neat and prompt execution of all kinds of Plain and Fancy Typography.

The Assortment of Type in this Office for General Printing is probably the largest in the country, comprising nearly

ONE THOUSAND

Distinct kinds of every Description of Plain, Fancy, and Ornamental

Types, Borders & Ornaments,

for every conceivable variety of work, from the Smallest Card or Label to the Largest Bill or Poster. In addition to this magnificent display of Type, the proprietors possess a complete

Gallery of Designs,

EMBRACING OVER

Two Thousand Different Engravings,

adapted for almost every purpose of Illustration—an advantage not possessed to the same extent by any other Establishment in this Country or in Europe.

PRINTING-HOUSE SQUARE—JUNCTION OF PARK ROW, NASSAU & SPRUCE STS.

The Steam Presses,

AND OTHER MACHINERY,

are all of the most recent and best patents for all kinds of

Fine Book, Wood-Cut, Newspaper, Job, Card, and Poster Printing.

THE PREMISES,

occupying the larger part of the Tribune Buildings, are probably unsurpassed in Location, for Light, and General Convenience, and enable the Proprietors to carry on all the various departments of their business with Celerity, System and Economy.

The Proprietors assure their old patrons and the public that they are as ambitious as ever to sustain the reputation of their Establishment for "GOOD WORK;" and they are determined to spare no pains to still further advance the character of the Art to which they have been so long and so successfully devoted.

BAKER & GODWIN, Book, Newspaper, Job, and Card Printers,

Printing-House Square, Opposite City Hall, N. Y.

C. & D. COOK & CO.

No. 140.

Fine Shifting Quarter Rockaway.

The Peck, Smith Manufacturing Co.

MANUFACTURERS OF

TINMEN'S MACHINES AND TOOLS,

STEEL TRAPS, STEEL YARDS,

Spoons, Pat. Screw Wrenches, Friction Rollers for Grindstones,

CHAIN PUMP ELEVATORS,

Saw Stretchers, Gate Hinges, Latches, Meat Cutters, Castors, Frying Pans, Sash Fasteners,

CUPBOARD CATCHES, &c., &c.

Manufactory on the Canal Railroad, at Southington, Center Station,

21 miles from New Haven, 97 miles, per Railroad, from New York.

WAREHOUSE, 58 BEEKMAN STREET, NEW YORK.

All communications should be addressed to SOUTHINGTON, CONN.

No. 141.

LIGHT FOUR SEAT ROCKAWAY.

AWARDED TO G. & D. Cook & Co. New Haven Ct. For BEST exhibition of Carriages. 1857.

AWARDED TO G. & D. Cook & Co. N. H. For best Carriages 1859.

GOLD.

AMERICAN INSTITUTE NEW-YORK

CONN. STATE AGRICULTURAL SOCIETY INCORP. 1852

GOLD.

WE have, during the past five years, exhibited our Carriages at very many Fairs and Exhibitions, in competition with other manufacturers, and have in every case received the highest prizes.

—:o:—

(*From the New Haven Palladium, Oct.,* 1859.)

We publish below a statement of the Committee appointed to examine the exhibition of carriages made by Messrs. G. & D. Cook & Co., at the State Fair. It will be seen that the Committee speak in the highest terms of the workmanship of this enterprising firm, and award them a good share of the prizes.

The report is as follows :

"Messrs. G. & D. Cook & Co. have fitted up a very large tent, where they make a beautiful display of Carriages, some twenty-two different and distinct styles, ALL of which are very fine, and well worthy of a premium ; in point of style and workmanship we have never seen them excelled. We therefore award them—

For Best Top Buggy, Diploma.
" Open "
" Pleasure Wagon, "
" Sleigh, "
" Chaise,

Which is all we have power to do according to the premium list. We would, however, inasmuch as they have shown many varieties not enumerated on the premium list (which are really worthy of some notice), recommend that the Society award them a Gold Medal for best Carriages.

RUSSELL TOMLINSON,
NELSON ALFORD,
S. N. HART,
Committee on Carriages."

(A Gold Medal was awarded.)

The above-named gentlemen are all first-class carriage makers, and proprietors of extensive manufactories in different parts of the State.

No. 142.

Turn Over Seat Rockaway.

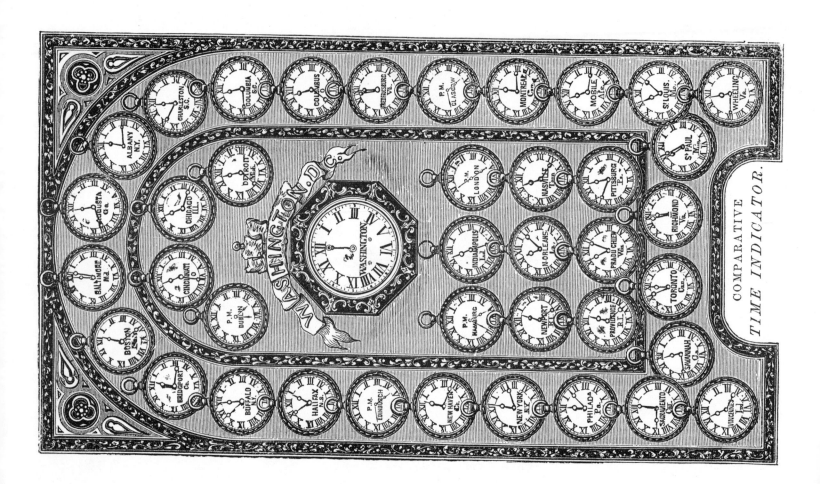

COMPARATIVE TIME INDICATOR.

No. 143.

LIGHT PERCH COACH.

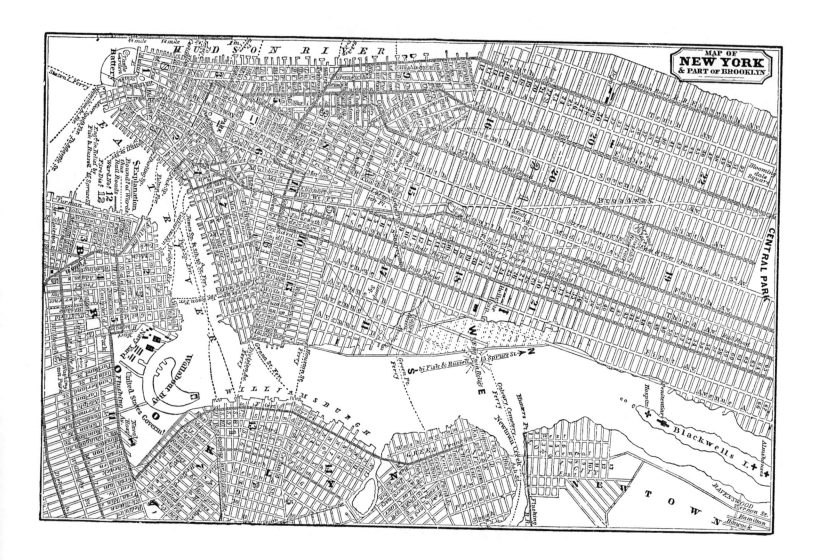

MAP OF
NEW YORK
& PART OF BROOKLYN

NEW HAVEN GREEN.

G. & D. COOK & CO.

No. 145.

New Orleans Charriottee.

G. & D. COOK & CO.

No. 145.

New Orleans Charriottee.

NEW HAVEN GREEN.

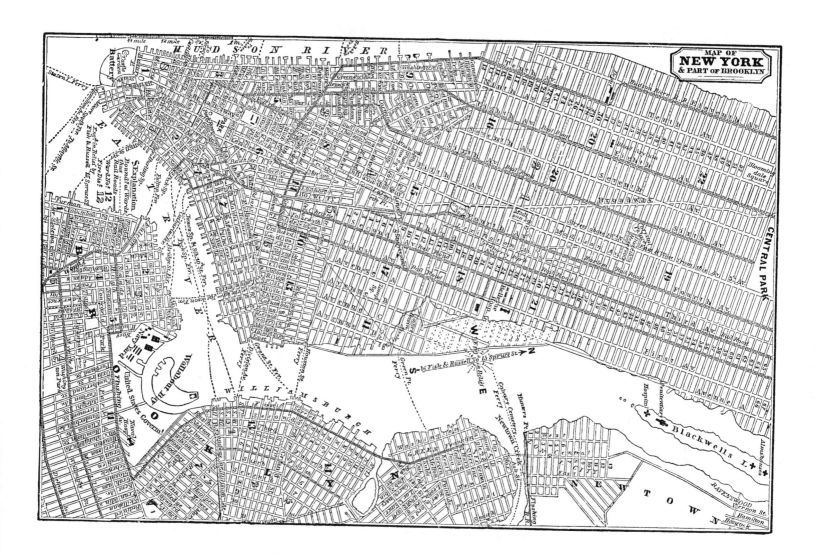

MAP OF
NEW YORK
& PART OF BROOKLYN

No. 143.

LIGHT PERCH COACH.

NEW HAVEN IN 1860.

A FEW NOTES BY A BUSINESS MAN WHO LOVES THE TOWN.

NEW HAVEN is to-day a city of more than forty thousand inhabitants, remarkable, as New Englanders generally are, alike for their ingenious industry, their enterprising, careful thrift, their shrewd, practical, cultivated sense, and their large aggregate wealth. It is said that at a wonderfully precocious age, and with an eye that has "*speculation*" in it, these people calculate the cost of all raw material, and the price of every article that can possibly be manufactured from it; and it is said, moreover, that a Yankee baby always invents a new *cradle* before he finally quits that "*institution!*"

With forty thousand such people, it is by no means strange that New Haven is now growing like a city in the west. See these figures a moment. New Haven was settled in 1638; was incorporated as a city in 1784. Its population in 1830 was only 10,678; in 1840, 14,390; in 1850, 22,529; in 1855, 31,549; in 1860, it is estimated as high as 44,000.

Its wealth has increased in still greater ratio:

1830	No. of Dwelling Houses		925	Assessed value of Property,		$2,639,353
1840	"	"	"	1,702	"	"	"	5,482,184
1845	"	"	"	2,223	"	"	"	6,087,877
1850	"	"	"	2,855	"	"	"	12,720,411
1855	"	"	"	3,844	"	"	"	20,960,590
1860	"	"	"	4,589	Estimated "	"	27,480,806

Its Location.

NEW HAVEN is situated seventy-six miles from New York, and about one hundred and twenty from Boston, on the line of both the direct inland routes between those two cities, and on the northerly shore of a fine broad bay, that extends some four miles up from Long Island Sound, and affords a spacious and convenient harbor for vessels drawing not more than sixteen feet of water. Its situation, in relation to Boston and New York, will be seen by the following cut of the Railroad and Steamboat routes.

The cut on the next page represents the more recently established, yet popular through route between Boston and New York, significantly called the "Shore Line."

This route commends itself especially to the man of business, with whom the saving of time is an object of importance; it being in advance of other lines in this particular. Also to the tourist of pleasure, running as it does along the shores of Long Island Sound, crossing the Connecticut River at Saybrook, and the Thames at New London, skirting the shores of the beautiful Narraganset Bay, (upon which is situated "Newport," the far-famed watering place,) the intermingling of cultivated fields and forest, sun and shade, with glimpses of the sea and shore, as the car glides steadily on through the soft sea breeze, being almost entirely free, at all seasons of the year, from *dust*, so annoying to travelers; thus forming a most speedy and delightful route between New York and Boston.

The road is thoroughly built, well supplied with easy and beautiful cars, well managed, and is rapidly increasing in heavy freights, as well as in the through passenger traffic. Over the Railroad from

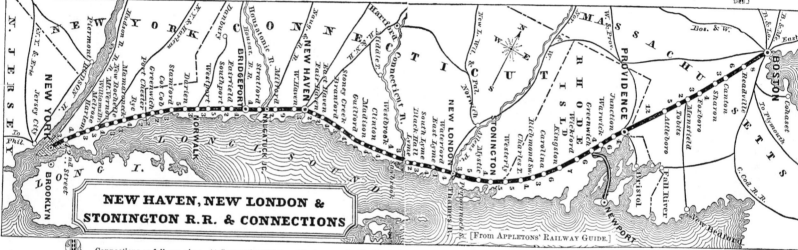

NEW HAVEN, NEW LONDON & STONINGTON R.R. & CONNECTIONS

[From Appletons' Railway Guide.]

Connections as follows, viz.:—At Connecticut River, with steamers for Hartford, Sag Harbor, and other points on the River and Sound; at New London, with railway for Norwich, Worcester, and vicinity; at East Greenwich, with the fast-sailing steamer Golden Gate, for Newport. Passengers from New York for Providence and Newport, will save from two to three hours time by taking this route.

New Haven to New York, six passenger trains pass each way daily, conveying multitudes to their destination; and yet in summer other multitudes take the cool, delightful Steamboats on the Sound, far from the noise and dust of the cars, and lose but little in time. The time by Railroad is about three hours, fare $1,65; by the Boat about five hours, fare $1. Boats start from New York at 3, and 11 p.m.; the cars at different hours, for which see Appleton's Railroad Guide.

Sailing Vessels.

There are also Sailing Packets plying with considerable regularity to and from Albany, New York, Philadelphia, Boston, Barbadoes, and the Windward Islands; and single vessels are almost daily arriving from and departing to all the more important ports of the world.

Public Carriages.

On reaching New Haven, your attention will certainly be at first attracted by the elegance of the public hacks, and agreeably surprised by the general civility of the drivers. They sometimes, however, will be none the less polite, if you remember that their legal charges are twenty-five cents a passenger for any distance less than a mile, and 12 cents for each additional half mile within the city limits, or one dollar per hour.

Hotels.

The Hotels in New Haven are equal in every respect to those of any other city. Among the best we might name the Tontine, and the New Haven House, both fronting the Park, and affording elegant and luxurious accommodations at a moderate rate. The Union House, the Merchants, and the City Hotel, all situated near the Depot in the center of the city, are good houses, and well kept. There are other hotels of less note, which give good fare at a somewhat cheaper rate, for which see City Directory.

After reaching your hotel, through quiet avenues shaded with the most magnificent and graceful Elms with which a city was ever adorned, you will assuredly remember that New Haven has long been known as the "City of Elms," as the seat of Yale College, and as *the most beautiful city in America.*

We know not how we can better describe it, than in the language of Dr. Meredith Reese, in a recent article published immediately after a visit to our city. Dr. Reese says:

"New Haven must be regarded as one of the most beautiful cities in the country, if not in the world. The private palatial residences of our public men, including those of our brethren there, have an air of quiet comfort, ample space, rural and architectural elegance, and horticultural adornment, to which we who are pent up in large cities cannot aspire. The luxuriant Elms which flourish in the parks and avenues which surround and beautify the classic groves and shades of Old Yale, give rare attraction to the eye of those who visit this Elm City for the first time, and make such in our toilsome profession sigh for that *otium cum dignitate,* which is the ultimatum of earthly ambition to most of us."

Carriage Manufacturers.

New Haven is also a city of large manufacturing interests. It is, indeed, the chief seat in America of the trade in Carriages. There are over sixty establishments in this city for the manufacture of carriages of different kinds. Many of them are of great extent and completeness, and turn out work justly celebrated for its elegance and substantial value wherever carriages are known. The largest and most complete in all its details and arrangements is that of Messrs. G. & D. Cook & Co., which is the largest carriage manufactory in the world, and turns out a carriage completely finished for the market every hour. Indeed, no other city, we are confident, can present half so wide a variety of general excellence and beauty in carriages as this. No other city—not even New York, which is itself largely supplied from New Haven—presents half so many inducements as this city, for purchasers and dealers to call and examine goods and prices.

Carriages from this city are to-day rolling in all parts of the United States, in Mexico, the West Indies, in Central and South

America. It is rapidly coming to be felt that New Haven is to the carriage trade what Nantucket and New Bedford are to the whale fishery, Lynn to the shoe trade, and Lowell and Manchester to the trade in cotton goods; so that no dealer can now afford to depend upon any other place for his larger supplies.

Other Manufactures.

The persevering genius and enterprise of its people has made New Haven, in a variety of *other* ways, prominent in industrial pursuits. Mr. Whitney, the inventor of the cotton gin, which has done so much to make cotton "king" in the financial world; Mr. Goodyear, who has added millions to the wealth of mankind in fabrics of India rubber; and Mr. Gold, the inventor, among many other things, of the steam heating apparatus, represent their inventive capacity; while Brewster, Cook, Collis, Jerome, Winchester, Trowbridge, Sheffield, Candee, and Whitney illustrate their tireless and comprehensive enterprise.

We hurriedly specify a few of the other larger branches of industry. A large manufactory of fabrics of India rubber is in successful operation. A manufactory of brass clocks—the largest in the world—has for a long time been established, where every day are made, completely finished, ready for the market, seven hundred clocks. There are here extensive establishments for the manufacture of all kinds of carriage goods; also, shirts, locks, fire-arms, shoes, furniture, clothing, builders' hardware, iron castings, machinery, daguerreotype cases, plated goods, and, in short, nearly every variety of manufactured articles known in the market may here be bought direct, at manufacturers' prices.

West India Trade.

With the West Indies, New Haven has always had an extensive and profitable trade. Horses, mules, and manufactured articles are the chief exports. The imports are sugar, molasses, rum, and tropical fruits. The trade of Barbadoes and the Windward Islands, with America, is chiefly done through this port.

But, although so much and so large a variety of business is carried on here, the whole air and spirit of the town is peculiarly graceful, quiet, and pleasant. You are at first everywhere struck with the grateful absence of noise, and smoke, and hurry. Every carriage runs so silently; every street is so clothed, and shaded, and adorned with the most graceful of trees; almost every house has such an air of quiet comfort, such a tasteful home-look, that you involuntarily think of scholars, and books, and the retirement of beautiful homes and quiet lives. You feel that the rattle, and fret, and worry of other towns has in some way floated off, when you enter upon these muffled and charmed streets.

Literary Institutions.

The most important of the literary institutions of the city is Yale College, with its various buildings, all surrounded with the majestic elms for which New Haven is celebrated. The College was originally founded at Killingworth, in the year 1700. It was chartered in 1701. In 1707 it was removed to Saybrook, and in 1716 it was removed to New Haven. Fronting on College Street, it has a row of eight brick buildings, five of which are four stories high. The remaining three are the Chapel, the Observatory, and the Lyceum, two of them with spires and one with a tower. In the rear of these are other College buildings—two of them being splendid specimens of architecture, namely, the College Library, which is one hundred and fifty feet in length, and Alumni Hall, used for public gatherings and College Society purposes. There are also the buildings known as the Chemical Laboratory, the Trumbull Gallery of Paintings, and the Mineralogical Cabinet building. Besides the academic course, there is a Law, a Medical, and a Theological department, and also a School of Philosophy and the Arts, in either of which, degrees may be obtained by diligent students.

The Schools.

New Haven is as celebrated for her Schools as for her Carriages. They consist of Seminaries for young ladies, Classical Schools for boys, which have a high character for discipline and efficiency, and they contain pupils from all the States in the Union, the Sandwich Islands, and other parts of the world. There are also thirteen Public Schools—nearly all of which are thoroughly graded and in successful operation,—where education is free and thorough.

The Colleges and Schools are interesting, on many accounts, to all. The fame of many scholars and statesmen is associated forever with these shady walks and with these "emerald domes." Among these libraries, quick young brains have grown bright and strong. In these cabinets of natural history, hints have become discovered facts, and laws so understood as to bless mankind with new wealth and power. In the picture gallery, and the scenery about the town, glimpses of beauty have given a new impetus to the cultivation of taste.

Carriage Drives.

The drives in the suburbs are of very great extent and variety. We can only indicate a few. First of all, you will want to climb the two mountains—East and West Rocks—that overlook the town,

"Twin giants guarding sea and land."

These are, in fact, the abrupt termination, on the south, of the Green Mountain range. On the top of "East Rock"—easily accessible with carriages—is a superb view and a good hotel, much frequented by strangers and lovers of the picturesque. To the elevation of this Rock you will love to steal away quietly, and gaze for hours on the boundless stretch of landscape before you—on the mountain streams and large rolling rivers, now dwindled to fairy ribbons, curling to the sea—on the town, nestled quietly among this thick, shady grove below you—on the country, for miles around dotted with white cottages and ample barns—on the blue shimmering sea, flecked with a hundred sails. West Rock, with its wintergreen falls, its wild glens and Judges' Cave (celebrated as the temporary abiding place of two of the judges—Whally and Goff—who condemned Charles I., and who were driven into exile at the Restoration), and the pretty little shady hamlet of Westville, at its foot, attracts many delighted visitors to its peculiar freshness and beauty.

Beyond Allentown, two miles to the southwest, is Prospect Hill, commanding a full view of the City and the Sound. It was here that Lieut. Campbell, of the British army, who fell in the last war, was buried. Some traces of his grave are still to be seen.

To Fair Haven and the heights beyond it; to the Forts, Hale and Beacon; to the Light House, "South End," "Double Beach," Branford Point, East Haven, Whitneyville, Whitney Avenue, Hillhouse Avenue, Highland Park, Brewster Park, Evergreen Cemetery, City Cemetery,—these are the most picturesque and charming drives. We ought not to omit many other places equally pleasant. Indeed, we cannot pass by "Lake Saltonstall," which has been described as "set in amongst steep hills covered with verdure to the water's edge—a lonely, lovely spot." Indeed, you can hardly go amiss about the town in any direction.

Brewster Park.

This is a beautiful plot of ground of about fifty acres, purchased and prepared for carriage drives and pedestrian strolls. It is enclosed with a high fence, has a carriage road all around it, with a fine trotting course of a mile in circuit, near the center of the Park. The place is daily thronged with citizens and their guests. It is about a mile from the Green, and is reached over a macadamized road.

Fishing.

To the disciples of Nimrod—the mighty hunter—we offer no grizzly bears, tigers, or wolves; only duck, quail, woodcock, rabbit, and the smaller game. There are fine brook trout, however, as coy and beautiful as ever flashed in a mountain stream. Bring along your "fly."

Summer Resorts.

Sachem's Head and Savin Rock—both in the neighborhood of New Haven—are celebrated as watering places. At Sachem's Head, a large and well-arranged hotel is kept, by H. Lee Scranton, the popular keeper of the Tontine Hotel in New Haven, and is designed for the residence of families and of pleasure parties during the summer months. At Savin Rock, "mine host" Upson dispenses to parties, winter and summer, all the delicacies and luxuries of all seasons and all climes. At both, plenty of company, and the best bathing, sailing, fishing, and sea food await the coming of the idle pleasure-seeker and the weary man of business.

And these drives along the shore and over the uplands—the watering places near—the variety, bounty, and delicacy of the sea food—the gayety of crowded and fashionable saloons, or of pleasure parties on the sound—the quiet beauty of New England homes on the shore of the "many-voiced" sea, all have a certain fascination for whoever has once come within the circle of their influence. Every convenience and comfort of elegant city or country life are here brought together, and, with the foregoing information, you can best judge whether a visit to this "Rural Queen of the East" can be made profitable and pleasant to you.

CARRIAGE MANUFACTURING.

No branch of business, with which we are conversant, has more rapidly developed itself in the last twenty years, or attained higher rank among the great manufacturing interests of the country, than that indicated in the heading of this article.

Twenty years ago the economical mechanic, or the staid, prudent farmer, would have considered the keeping of a pleasure carriage an unwarrantable luxury, justly subjecting him to the charge of extravagance. Those who were obliged to have some kind of a vehicle, could afford nothing better than the square box wagon, set flat upon rough wooden axles, and in many instances with no other seat than a board thrown across the top of the body. And this must be used upon all occasions, and for all purposes, whether to carry the family to meeting, the grist to the mill, or the pork and poultry to market. But gradually, as the facilities for the manufacture of carriages have increased, thereby reducing their cost, this state of things has undergone a wonderful change; and to-day, could the farmer of twenty years ago visit the carriage-house of almost any of our thriving mechanics or well-to-do farmers, he would scarcely believe his own eyes; there he would behold, instead of the clumsy, jolting box wagon, in which he used to ride, a genteel business wagon, tastefully painted, with good iron (case-hardened) axles, fine English steel-tempered springs, and with a roomy, comfortable seat, well-trimmed and cushioned; in addition to this he would find a nice top buggy, and in some instances a fine Rockaway, or a luxurious coach; in short, a pleasure-carriage of some kind has become as indispensable as a good horse.

From among the many carriage manufacturers whose success has tended to produce this great change, we select one to illustrate our subject.

We give a partial view of the premises of Messrs. G. & D. Cook & Co., carriage manufacturers, New Haven, Conn.* This firm commenced business about nine years since, in a small shop, at the corner of Grove and State Streets, New Haven, where their present large and commodious establishment now stands. At the commencement of their business they adopted a principle entirely novel among carriage-makers, viz.: that of systematizing, dividing, and sub-dividing their work, in such a manner that each man had but a single part to perform, thereby enabling him to learn it to such perfection that he could execute it very rapidly and at a great reduction of cost. One can readily conceive of the advantage this system would give them over their competitors, who performed their work after the old plan—each man performing all the different parts in turn until the carriage was completed. The successful operation of their system enabled them to turn out one carriage per day, which at that time was considered a wonderful achievement, and soon attracted the general attention of the craft. This well-known firm now complete, by the same system, no less than *ten per day*, with the same ease and success with which they could

*See frontispiece of this edition.

then complete one per day. Their original factory was a single building fifty feet by twenty feet, two stories in height, giving them with the basement about 3,000 square feet of floor-room, which has since increased to the immense proportions shown in the picture, increasing their floor-room from 3,000 to over 85,000 square feet—equal to a one-story building covering *two acres* of ground.

Under the system referred to, this factory is now divided into twenty-four separate departments, covering everything appertaining to the making and shipping of a carriage, each department being under the control of a competent foreman.

All orders are first examined by Mr. Kimball (one of the proprietors), and arranged by him upon blanks prepared for the purpose, stating *definitely* the style and finish (even to the *minutest points*) of each job ordered, and also, when it is to be completed, then given out to each foreman, and he is held *personally responsible* for the faithful execution of the portion under his supervision.

This establishment now gives employment to over three hundred workmen, and in addition to this force they have a beautiful and powerful steam-engine, every revolution of whose ponderous wheel gives life and activity to over fifty beautifully working machines, adapted to almost any conceivable part of their work, performing an amount of work equal to the whole number of their men, and with far greater accuracy than can possibly be done by hand labor. When we look at this powerful array of forces, we no longer wonder that their elegant pleasure-wagons are completed at the rate of one per hour, and even then not keeping pace with their orders, which their tasty, well-finished, and durable carriages, no less than the superiority of their work and their liberal advertisements, scattered broadcast over the land in the form of newspapers, books, charts, descriptive catalogues, etc., have brought them from almost all parts of the habitable globe where carriage wheels have rolled, making the name of G. & D. Cook & Co., not only in New Haven, but in every city and town in the Union, as "familiar as household words."

Should you visit the establishment of the Messrs. Cook, you will always find some one of their firm ready to attend to your wants, and to conduct you through all the departments of their mammoth factory, explaining the operations of all the numerous machines, from the delicate sewing machine (of which they have some dozen in the trimming department) to the huge monster who stands near the entrance to the basement, puffing from his powerful iron lungs the breath which keeps alive the numerous forge-fires in their immense blacksmith's shop. And should you be unable to find among the many varieties of their manufacture (which number not less than fifty) a carriage just suited to your taste, they will take you in their carriage from shop to shop, among their brother carriage-makers, until you have found the style you seek. This cordiality is highly appreciated by their customers and visitors; the liberal course they have ever pursued, together with the taste, skill, and talent manifested in all their operations, have made the firm the well-known favorite of the carriage-dealers and consumers throughout the country.